SNACKS FOR DINNER

Small Bites, Full Plates, Can't Lose

Lukas Volger

Photography by Cara Howe

HARPER WAVE
An Imprint of HarperCollinsPublishers

SNACKS FOR DINNER

HarperCollins books may be purchased for educational, business, or sales promotional use. For information, please email the Special Markets Department at SPsales@harpercollins.com.

FIRST EDITION

Designed by Bonni Leon-Berman
Photography by Cara Howe
Wedding photography by Emmanuel Rosario

Library of Congress Cataloging-in-Publication Data has been applied for.

ISBN 978-0-06-314322-7

22 23 24 25 26   TC   10 9 8 7 6 5 4 3 2 1

FOR (and with) VINCENT

CONTENTS

SNACKS FOR DINNER

INTRODUCTION | Leslie's Lunch

I was a week into my vacation, traveling up the California coast, exploring with abandon, meeting with friends, teaching a few cooking classes, and eating nearly all my meals out. It was a bit of a blowout, but like any good vacation, it didn't necessarily feel that way at the time. On this particular afternoon, I knew only that one of my favorite family friends, Leslie Wooley, had invited my husband, Vincent, and me over for lunch.

I'm going to the farmers' market in the morning, she'd texted me as we were confirming the time, *so I'll just grab a few goodies.* At noon, we headed her way.

When we arrived, things looked . . . well, not quite ready. My cooking style is rarely very fussy, but if I'm having people over, even if it's just an informal lunch, I do some planning. I decide on the menu ahead of time, prep what can be prepped, clear the table, and arrange the napkins and utensils. I try to get myself to a place where, by the time my guests arrive, I won't be distracted by the kind of cooking that'll require my full focus. But at Leslie's house, no such prep was visible. A newspaper was still spread out over the dining table along with remnants of the day's errand-making, and the kitchen showed no signs of any activity.

But as we started to catch up, Leslie cleared away the table, rummaged through her refrigerator, and in a matter of minutes set out what would be our lunch. It featured little half-pints of prepared salads and dips, a bag of crackers emptied into a bowl, two different wedges of cheese on a plate alongside a butter knife. On another plate, she piled a few carrots and cucumbers that she washed and chopped as we chatted.

It didn't look like something that I'd immortalize in my recipe journal, but as we sat down and started eating—I wondered why this was such a pleasant and satisfying meal. Was it because it was a contrast to all the rich restaurant food we'd been eating? Was it that each element of the meal—the tabbouleh from the farmers' market, straight from the half-pint it was sold in, the slab of Havarti cheese, the juicy and crunchy farm-fresh carrots—was just effortlessly delicious on its own? What was the secret to these . . . these snacks? We devoured everything.

In the weeks and months that followed, Vincent and I talked about Leslie's lunch countless times. Sometimes intentionally, but oftentimes subconsciously, I sought to re-create it, particularly as the COVID-19 pandemic began gripping our lives and mandating extra-resourceful cooking at home. I'd rummage through the fridge to set out a few dips I'd made or bought along with crackers, or slices of grilled bread, a plate of thoughtfully cut-up vegetables, a bowl of what I now think of as a "spoon salad," and maybe a couple boiled eggs sprinkled with a seasoned salt or dabs of mustard—and this was dinner! It always felt surprisingly festive, like apero or aperitivo—little bites of a few different things, none of it individually plated, all placed at the center of the table for the sharing—but also satisfying and complete. And it stuck, as you can see from the book you're holding in your hands, completely shaking up the way I think about dinner.

HOW IT WORKS

The chapters in *Snacks for Dinner* are essentially organized by trait. Each one represents an important component of a snacky dinner, bringing together textures, flavors, and degrees of heartiness to create a satisfying, balanced meal:

- CRISPY-CRUNCHY | SAVORY, SNACKY BITES

- TANGY-JUICY | PICKLES + MARINADES

- SCOOPED + SMEARED | DIPS + SPREADS

- CENTERPIECE-ISH | A LITTLE HEARTIER

- SMALL BUT MIGHTY | SALADS + SOUPS

- STURDY SUPPORT | CRACKERS, BREADS, CHIPS

- SIPS + SWEETS | DRINKS + DESSERTS

Not every single category needs to be represented in a single meal, but most of them ought to. You might start with a few handfuls of toasted nuts or a fun snack mix such as Smoky Glazed Pistachios (page 40) or Chex Snack Mix Revisited (page 39) for the crispy-crunchy element. You could add some zesty dressed vegetables and pickles such as Orange + Mustard Marinated Asparagus (page 67) with Honeyed Pickled Shallots (page 62) to cover your tangy-juicy component. A bowl of something that can be scooped and smeared, such as Toasted Walnut + Feta Dip (page 83), would go nicely here, along with an accompanying vessel such as Salt + Pepper Wheat Crackers (page 190)—which also add a little extra padding to the meal. Perhaps you round this out with something small but mighty, such as a fresh little salad with some nutritional density—the Lentils, Carrots + Dates with Dill (page 160) would be perfect— and a few boiled eggs seasoned at the table with a pinch of a Herby Seasoning Blend (page 123) tucked into a nice platter of raw veggies for snacking and dipping—and you've got dinner.

You could also start with something a little centerpiece-ish like the beautiful Feta + Jam Tart (page 117), and build a meal with Oyster Mushrooms in Walnut Oil (page 68), some Lemony Fried Chickpeas (page 49) for salty crunch, and the rich-but-hearty Dill + White Bean Spread (page 106) to accompany the Gluten-Free Nut + Seed Crackers (page 194). The Roasted Radish + Grapefruit Salad (page 156), a juicy dish, completes a dazzling spread. You'll find dozens of such suggestions for menus like this throughout this book.

One thing I particularly like about these meals is how they shake up the traditional composition of a protein plus two sides by diversifying the plate with smaller amounts of different foods. It's a style of eating that especially makes sense for vegetarian and vegan cooking. The food is fun and satisfying, and nutritional balance happens easily. In fact, this approach decenters the "filler"—starchy stuff like grains, pasta, or bread—in favor of more vegetables. Snacky-style eating offers an opportunity to expand vegetable offerings, in the form of a beautiful platter of enticing vegetables, or in dips and spreads, bright quick pickles, and intriguing textured salads. You can get a lot of vegetables onto the table this way, and it all looks so exciting that no one ever feels deprived.

MAKE-AHEAD + STORE-BOUGHT

Throwing around these menus as if a snacky meal really is so effortless to whip up—I can feel you narrowing your eyes at me. *He said this was about simplifying things. This sounds like a lot of work.* I do promise that ease is a guiding principle of these meals, and not only are the vast majority of the recipes quite easy, many of them can be made in advance. So when it comes time to pull together a quick weeknight dinner, it's more a matter of assembly than cooking.

Let me also say that in the spirit of a weeknight dinner of snacks, it's implied that some of the items on the table will have been procured elsewhere. Not everything must be homemade. I certainly take advantage of the amazing food purveyors in my community—picking up a dip or spread here, a pickle or spoon salad there—and I encourage you to do the same. I know you'll be able to find what you need by shopping at your nearest chain grocery store, but I strongly encourage you to source locally whenever possible, and strive to support the markets and makers in your community. You may already know just where to look, but if you're in need of inspiration, here are a few of my favorite sources:

- **The Farmers' Market:** When I visit markets across the country, I often find stands offering breads and pastries; pickles, jams, and other preserves; and prepared foods like salads, dips, and spreads. (There's even a farm stand at my local market that sells fresh-made potato chips!) It's always a good idea to start your shopping there.

- **Specialty Shops:** A good cheese shop, which is of course a terrific resource for both locally made and imported cheeses that are fresh and/or properly stored, can also be a great place to find olives, jams, and pickles as well. And don't skip over markets that cater to non-Western cuisines, like Indian, Asian, and Middle Eastern groceries. You'll find there all kinds of great snacks-for-dinner stuff, like dips, pickles, breads, and various salads and prepared vegetables, plus crunchy snacks and snack mixes, too.

- **Local Bakeries and Pastry Shops:** In my midtwenties, developing a "bread routine" was one of the things that made me feel like a grown-up. To this day, most every weekend I head to my favorite bread bakery of the moment for the week's loaf, which I slice up and store in the freezer for snacking on all week long. In addition, international bakeries—Lebanese and Middle Eastern ones in particular—may have freshly made flatbreads and wonderful, easy-to-snack-on desserts. Bakeries and pastry shops can also be resources for savory tarts, fun and freshly made crackers, spiced nuts, and much more.

- **Microbakeries:** When COVID-19 hit the restaurant industry like a tidal wave, many pastry chefs and bread bakers supported themselves by becoming one-person small businesses, selling their creations on their own. These types of shops can be a particularly fun option for desserts, but are also a great option for bread and crackers. Instagram is often the best resource for discovering home bakeries in your area.

SNACKY DINNER PARTIES

I'm not a big fan of using the word "elevated" in reference to food—so often it's a coded dig with a questionable subtext, such as when tacos or Southern mac 'n' cheese is described that way—but part of me wants to frame these recipes as "elevated snacks," because their colorful, fun nature makes them worth showing off. As much as I love on-the-fly weeknight snack dinners, sharing these meals with friends and family is one of my favorite ways to enjoy all the recipes collected here. Furthermore, it allows for easy accommodation of dietary preferences and restrictions. Similar to a build-your-own grain or vegetable bowl, everyone at the table can customize their own plates.

That said, when sharing a snacky dinner with a crowd, I do put some more time and effort into the preparation. A few days before I have guests over, I'll jot down a menu that might be a teeny bit more ambitious than usual, planning so that I can share, say, My Ideal Focaccia (page 185), which requires a good 24 to 48 hours of rising in the refrigerator, a salad or two, a soup to serve in little cups, as well as an array of pickles, marinades, crackers, and some fun savory, crunchy bites. Maybe a colorful tart to anchor the meal. As I said, most everything can be made in advance, so as far as entertaining goes, these recipes offer a great way to front-load all of the work.

Then I set everything out on the table. Maybe I'll go for a cocktail party vibe, with movement and fluidity as people mingle standing up, or eat cross-legged on the floor around the coffee table. It's also just as much fun to eat at the dining table, with candles and a full setting, where I can enjoy watching my friends and family pick through the assorted dishes over a long, lingering meal. Give it a try—it's impossible not to enjoy. (And if you need some help with the music, I've got a snacky dinner playlist on my website: lukasvolger.com/playlist.)

It is my wish that rethinking dinner in this way serves to lighten the mental load of meal planning, allowing it to be intentionally informal rather than passively so (as a dinner of dips and crackers might otherwise seem). I also hope that giving you permission (and practical instruction) to rethink traditional notions of entertaining inspires you to bring together your friends and family for gatherings more often. It's no less exciting and impressive than a more regimented sit-down dinner—the fun assortment of snacks always dazzles, and the immediate invitation to dig in makes everyone feel openly welcome—but it's just so much easier to pull off, and it always allows me to spend more time *with* my friends and family, rather than project managing their experience. Last, I'll be happy if these recipes find their way into regular (read: not snacky) dinners, too—they're flexible that way.

But more than anything, I hope that *Snacks for Dinner* broadens your thinking about what exactly makes a meal, and gives you license to experiment and challenge your assumptions. At Leslie's lunch, she certainly didn't put on any airs about being revolutionary, but what an impact those humble little snacks had on me.

It's no secret that having the right tools and knowing the right tricks makes cooking a more pleasurable experience. Sometimes we put speed bumps in our kitchens that we're not even aware of, and when moments of insight arrive—*Oh,* that's *how you trim the peel off a grapefruit*—it has a ripple effect as you realize its range of applications. After all, tools and tricks aren't just about shortcuts and efficiency. They're also about ergonomics, and turning the physicality of cooking into something that feels natural and easy rather than clunky and hard.

This list isn't exhaustive, because I know that you know you'll need some basic cooking equipment, like skillets, a knife, and a cutting board. These are merely some of the tools and ingredients that might not be obvious, and that I think are worth highlighting in the context of making snacky meals.

TOOLS

FOOD PROCESSOR AND/OR A HIGH-SPEED BLENDER: I have a love-hate relationship with my food processor. Love, because it's so dang useful, and hate, because I find it to be one of the most tedious items in my kitchen to clean and to store. In my past cookbooks, I've always offered workarounds whenever possible for readers who don't own food processors, because when I was a younger cook I didn't have one, so recipes that required them always made me feel left out.

Unfortunately, a food processor is more necessary here than in most other cookbooks; it's kind of a dip essential. You can sometimes use a high-speed blender instead, but those often require more liquid to get the mixture moving than you need in a food processor, and scraping a thick dip out of a blender pitcher is also a chore. When there's a food processor workaround in these recipes, I always offer it.

I use my high-speed blender almost daily to make smoothies, but it's also an incredibly powerful tool for making smooth, velvety soups and nut- and seed-based nondairy milks, and you can even use it as a juicer, as I do in my Spicy Celery Margarita (page 206), by blending the solids and then straining them out. While its narrower design means it works differently than a food processor for pureeing thicker consistencies, such as dips and spreads, it can sometimes be substituted. And, in many cases, it produces a silkier dip or spread because it blends so smoothly; you'll just need to add more liquid than you would with a food processor.

Handheld immersion blenders and bullet-style blenders can be handy for smaller jobs, though I don't always find them to be as effective. The former is particularly useful for blending up soups, but isn't as thorough as a blender and doesn't really work for processing thicker dips and spreads. Bullet-style blenders are great for small-volume jobs and for chopping nuts or making dressings, and you can certainly use one to work in batches, but as a substitute for a food processor they aren't perfect, since they require more liquid to get the motors moving.

For both food processors and high-speed blenders, you can often find refurbished ones at a significant discount. eBay offers both, backed by a two-year warranty, and on Vitamix's website (vitamix.com) they also sell an array of refurbished blenders. And if you're ever gifted an older Cuisinart food processor, one made in the 1990s or early aughts, snatch it up. I still find their motors to be stronger and generally more durable than newer models.

> **Trick for Cleaning Your Food Processor and Blender:** Once you've rinsed out the bowl of the food processor or the blender pitcher, fill it with an inch or so of hot water and a few drops of dish soap, then process it for twenty to thirty seconds. This helps to dislodge some of the sticky bits from the blades and bottom edges, and also helps to get rid of any oily film.

QUARTER SHEET PANS: In restaurant lingo, what home cooks call a "baking sheet" is called a "half sheet"—as in, half of a sheet pan, where a full sheet pan is twice its size to fit inside an industrial-sized oven. You can probably guess what a quarter sheet pan is by this logic: it's half the size of a standard baking sheet, measuring 9 by 13 inches (22 by 33 centimeters). They're more lightweight, easier to store and clean, and somehow just infinitely more handy than a 9-by-13-inch glass baking dish. I use these a lot for setting up my "mise" when I'm cooking a few things at once, gathering all the ingredients for each recipe onto a quarter sheet pan so that I visualize and strategize what's on the cooking docket. But they're terrific for smaller baking jobs where a full baking sheet is more than you need: toasting nuts, small batches of granola, cooking a single eggplant, roasting vegetables, spreading out cooked greens or lentils to cool. And they're also the perfect size for baking off a double batch of brownies.

DIGITAL SCALE: If you've purchased a baking book in the last fifteen years, you've certainly been encouraged to get a digital scale—once you get into the habit of weighing your ingredients, you'll never want to go back to measuring cups. And in my baking recipes here, too, you'll have the best results by using a scale. In the recipes where I find the weight measurements to be more important, like My Ideal Focaccia (page 185), I prioritize that measurement in the ingredient list. But do you know what a digital scale is also great for? Checking the size of your vegetables! I realized when I observed some of the testing for this book that not everyone has an intuitive sense for what, say, a medium leek looks like. If you don't, your frame of reference becomes the other leeks at the grocery store on whatever day you go shopping, where they're all probably the same size. I've included weights for such vegetables, which means that if you can only find a large leek, or aren't sure what a medium leek looks like, you can weigh it at home and take the necessary steps in determining that you'll only need to use half of it. Just get yourself a digital scale. You won't regret it. Plus, you can get a perfectly good one for around $15.

STORAGE SOLUTIONS FOR SNACKS: This book largely came about from sticking my head in the refrigerator to see what odds and ends could be cobbled together to pass as dinner. Which is to say, it forced me to spend more time gazing at various food storage solutions than ever before, and realizing that they're an integral part of knowing how to cook resourcefully. Here are some of my favorite options.

- **Repurposed Glass Jars:** It doesn't take long to build up a supply of glass jars by simply reusing the ones that previously had mustard or jam or honey in them. To rid them of lingering smells, I simply fill them up with distilled white vinegar, let them soak for 30 to 60 minutes, then wash and air-dry. And most labels come off by scrubbing with a bit of steel wool under hot, soapy water. I use these to make vinaigrettes, to portion out soup, and as airtight containers for dry beans, grains, nuts, and leftover snack mixes.

- **Plastic Deli Containers:** Space-wise, I find these to be the most efficient of any storage container I've ever used. They stack well—both when empty and when full—and they're lightweight and inexpensive, and often exactly the right size (either pint or quart) that I need. You can buy them by the sleeve at restaurant supply stores, often at your local discount or dollar store, and plenty of places online.

- **Weck, Mason, or Other Canning Jars:** I ordered a case of Weck jars a year ago and am so glad I did. Pickles, pâtés, and even tisanes and other infusions always look so pretty in them. And it can be a relief and comfort, bringing order to your cupboards and fridge, when they all line up so nicely, all the same make and size. The canning jars I find to be most useful are the wide-mouthed ones, which are easier to fill than those that taper, and also safer for freezing.

- **Rectangular Food Storage Containers:** Not everything fits in a jar. Repurposed tins can work great for larger items like crackers if you don't need an absolutely airtight seal, but many brands make both glass and plastic containers. Plastic ones are more lightweight and stack neatly in your cupboard or drawers, but they can hold on to odors and stain; glass ones are heavier and don't stack well, but they're more heat-safe and much more resistant to smells and stains. A great perk of the glass ones is that they can double as baking dishes and even servingware. I find that I never need more than two of these, so I've built up a much larger supply of the smaller-sized containers instead.

- **Beeswax Wraps:** These are pieces of cloth in various sizes that have been dipped in wax to make them malleable, meant to be a sustainable alternative to disposable plastic wrap and aluminum foil. Odors from foods like onions can get trapped, but they're excellent for instances of sealing up a tray of blondies, or hunks of cheese, or half an avocado. And they can make a perfect substitute for plastic wrap when sealing up a disc of dough or pie crust to chill. When washing them, don't use super-hot water, as the wax will melt off.

- **Universal Silicone Lids:** These are simply flat discs made of silicone that, once set on top of a bowl or a saucepan, form an airtight seal. They're very handy for allowing bread dough to rise, and for saving leftovers that are in bowls that you don't want to transfer to a Tupperware.

A STONE OR STEEL FOR THE OVEN: An oven steel or stone—the kind used for making pizza—is just a slab of metal or ceramic stone that sits directly on one of your oven racks, or even in the bottom of the oven as long as it doesn't cover up a heat vent. For pizza, the idea is that when it's fully preheated, it can get closer to the temperature of a proper pizza oven's floor. But I hardly use mine for pizza. I just leave it in the oven on the center rack, where it helps to redistribute the oven heat and improves the browning on most foods. I find that everything just cooks more evenly, and the flat steel provides a smooth surface for sheet pans and whatnot.

A FEW MINI TOOLS: I used to think that the purpose of mini kitchen tools was just to clutter up your drawers. But I've done a 180 on that stance—now these are some of my favorite tools to reach for. The following are indispensable in my kitchen.

- **Small, Flexible Silicone Spatula:** The one I have is made by GIR, and I'm embarrassed to admit that every time I think, *I need a spatula,* and then remember that I'll get to use this particular one, I get excited. It's small enough to easily fit inside a jar of peanut butter, making it easy to scrape out the dregs stuck to the bottom of any jar, but big enough that you can still use it for scraping out the contents of a medium-sized bowl or for scrambling eggs.

- **Mini Offset Spatula:** Food stylists love these things, because they're the secret to billowy "swoops" of frosting, whipped cream, and whatnot. They're also a terrific tool for scraping the sides of a food processor bowl and for spreading batter evenly into a rimmed baking sheet or pan. And they're so thin that they're also perfect for tucking under the delicate edge of a cheese frico or transferring small cookies onto a cooling rack.

- **Small Flat Coil Whisk:** My mom gave me one of these when I moved off to live on my own, and it's still a tool that I'm glad to have. It's essentially a mini whisk where its coils are wrapped around a U-shaped piece of wire affixed to the handle. Its shape makes it easy to whisk right against the bottom or sides of a bowl, and thus very effective for small-volume jobs, and I also use it when whisking sauces in skillets and small saucepans—it's perfect for making a roux.

FINE-MESH SIEVES AND STRAINERS: My 7½-inch sieve is one of my most used items. I reach for it constantly to rinse rice and beans; strain stock, teas, and infusions; as a basket for squeezing homemade nut or seed milks; and to drain the whey from homemade ricotta. I also have a small one that's 3½ inches in diameter, and I use that almost as often—for similar things but smaller volumes. You can mimic a fine-mesh strainer by lining a colander with a few layers of cheesecloth, but it's much less of a hassle to just equip your kitchen with a proper one. There's no need to buy an expensive model, but do make sure that it has a sturdy frame and handle that won't bend to pressure, and that is securely fastened to the mesh strainer, so that it doesn't get pried loose over time.

SALAD SPINNER: The salad spinner is so ripe for a major overhaul (*why* are they so bulky and so prone to developing mold?!) and yet so essential, because if you eat a lot of vegetables you'll need to wash them. I use my salad spinner as often as a basket-lined basin for washing radishes, tomatoes, berries, and herbs as I do for lettuce. My favorite model is manufactured by Zyliss, and a reader of my blog once gave me the tip that after you've cleaned and towel-dried your spinner, you can spin it one final time to wring off the water trapped inside the spinning mechanism, which has helped somewhat to prevent mold. And if you don't have a salad spinner, my favorite method for drying greens is the one I learned from my grandpa: pile them on top of a clean kitchen towel, turn that into a bundle by holding it by the four corners, then go outside and spin it over your head helicopter-style. It's shockingly effective.

SERVINGWARE FOR SNACKS: I've accumulated a varied collection of plates, platters, boards, and bowls over the years, and very little of it matches. I prefer the variety it brings to the table, and having options when it comes time to plate foods. Here are a few tips on how I collect and utilize it.

- **Salad Plates and Shallow Soup Bowls:** These work great as servingware for dips and other snacks, just the ones that you probably already own. If your salad plate has a bit of a rim, even better—you can just scoop dip into the center of the plate, then smear it around using the back of a spoon (or a small offset spatula). These same dishes are also great for setting out sliced bread, crackers, and pickles. They're small enough that you can easily fit several of them on the table at once.

- **Clearance Racks and Discount Department Stores:** These can be good resources for individual pieces, particularly platters and boards, serving spoons and cheese knives, but also individual plates and bowls, too. I have a real weakness for places like Cost Plus World Market, which has fairly inexpensive servingware to begin with, as well as a robust clearance section. The same can be said for HomeGoods and other similar department stores.

- **Accent Pieces from Antique or Secondhand Stores:** I'm not as much of a second-hand shopper as I'd like to be, but in my dabbling I've happened upon some wonderful and distinctive bowls, platters, and plates. It's always helpful to not be wedded to the idea of a complete set, and instead pick up an item here and there, as you stumble on things you like.

- **Ceramics and Pottery:** Collect bowls, plates, and platters as you would art by buying them directly from ceramicists. One-of-a-kind pieces are expensive, of course, but as I said, they're art, and they can last a lifetime. Most ceramicists and potters also periodically throw what they call "seconds sales," which is when they sell all the inventory that's slightly imperfect at discount. A lot of what constitutes an imperfection for a professional ceramicist—a little nick or slight unevenness—goes right over my head, so for me these discounted pieces are as good as the real thing.

A FEW TRICKS + TIPS

TEMPERATURE SETTINGS ON YOUR STOVETOP: I've cooked these recipes in a few different kitchens, and it's a point of frustration that when trying to make a recipe fail-safe, every stovetop's heat settings are different, meaning that a "medium" heat setting is highly subjective. So, at risk of stating what may be painfully obvious, allow me to provide some visual cues for context:

- **High Heat:** If you add oil to a skillet heated up over high heat, it will immediately start to shimmer and smoke. When food goes into the pan, there's instant, audible searing. I don't use high heat very often for "dry" cooking, like searing and sautéing vegetables, because it's so easy to scorch your food and smoke out your kitchen. For me, this setting is primarily for bringing a pot of water to boil.

- **Medium-High Heat:** In a skillet placed over high heat, oil will start to shimmer almost instantly, but there shouldn't be any immediate smoking. Medium-high is my go-to for "quick" heat applications, like blistering or searing or browning the outsides of foods. Often, after some color is achieved, I'll reduce the heat so that the interiors of the food will cook more gently and thoroughly.

· **Medium Heat:** Medium heat should generate active simmering of sauces, a few notches below a boil but not *gentle*. Oil added to a pan over medium heat will loosen up a bit more slowly, but once food is added to it, there will still be audible sizzling. It's ideal for shallow-frying, and for cooking vegetables when you want a caramelized exterior and tender, cooked-through interior. Medium heat is, of course, the Goldilocks of heat levels.

· **Medium-Low Heat:** Medium-low is for gentle simmering—there will be a steady stream of bubbles around the perimeter of the pan if it's filled with water, but the water won't erupt into anything resembling a boil. When making polenta or tomato-based pasta sauces, this is the temperature setting for the bulk of the cooking. It's also the temperature for toasting whole spices.

· **Low Heat:** Low heat is for steaming rice and generally keeping things warm, but not producing any visible activity in the pan. I find low heat to be the hardest to meaningfully achieve on home stovetops, particularly gas ones—most that I've used have no problem getting searing hot, but there's very little range between a medium and a low flame. If your stovetop is the same, it may be useful to get a flame diffuser, which is just a slab of iron that you sandwich between your flame and your pan to soften and even out the heat application.

DON'T FORGET YOUR BROILER!: Think of your broiler as a giant toaster turned sideways, which means that it's great for making several pieces of toast at a time, but also that it's *the* tool to use for charring and blistering when you don't have access to an outdoor grill. My broiler at home looks like a drawer located at the very bottom of the oven, but other ovens have their broiler heat source located at the top of the oven. It's a great heat setting because there's not much of a preheat required—you're effectively just placing your food close to an open flame. I use it often for charring bell peppers and eggplant, but also sheet pans of roasted vegetables that didn't achieve as much cosmetic blistering as I'd like. Whenever you use your broiler, be sure to set a timer so that you don't turn your meal to blackened embers.

KEEPING HERBS FRESH: This isn't a new method, but it bears repeating: after you've washed and dried your herbs, spread them out on a clean towel or double layer of paper towels, and roll them up like a cigar. Then place that in an airtight container or bag. Stored this way, they'll likely keep for a week or more. This method also works great for salad greens.

WASHING YOUR CITRUS: There's a lot of citrus in this book—lemons, grapefruits, limes—and I love to incorporate its zest into recipes, since the citrus oils are located there and they can add the flavor of citrus without its acid. Because of the pesticides and fertilizers sprayed over conventional citrus, I opt for organic citrus when zesting. And most citrus sold at the grocery store, even the organic stuff, is waxed, so it's a good idea to give it a scrub.

NOTES ON A FEW PANTRY INGREDIENTS

FAT: Fat flows a bit more freely here than in my previous books, particularly in the form of olive oil drizzled over dips and salads. I think it's worth reiterating that fat is more than just moistness and mouthfeel, that it's also a medium for flavor. You can tinker with fat to balance a dish in the same way that you can tinker with salt and acid. For my recipes that involve frying, I've already cut back on the fat by shallow- rather than deep-frying, but for searing and sautéing, you can always reduce the amount as needed, and use a nonstick pan. But flavor will suffer a bit.

My fat of choice is almost exclusively olive oil. For most of my day-to-day cooking, I use organic olive oil that I buy at Costco or the California Olive Ranch brand, and for finishing, I belong to a wonderful "olive oil subscription" called Fat Gold, where four times a year I get a little tin of fresh, small-batch olive oil made from California olive groves, which is such a treat. I recommend keeping a bit of finishing olive oil on hand, as even a small amount can do a lot to enhance a dish. Buy it in small amounts, so that you use it up while it's still vibrant and fresh.

Additionally, since I use it so often, I keep my large tins or bottles of olive oil stowed away in a dark cupboard, where they stay cool, and then for easy access in day-to-day cooking, I decant it into a squeeze bottle that I keep on the countertop. (I love a squeeze bottle for oil!) Olive oil is more perishable that you might think, and can turn extra quickly when left in a place where it's exposed to sunlight (which heats it up).

VINEGAR: Once you build an understanding of all the different types of vinegars available, and their differing flavors and degrees of acidity, I think you'll find that it's a source of pride to have a cupboard shelf devoted to a bunch of different types of vinegars. My most used vinegars are apple cider vinegar; white, red, and sherry wine vinegar; rice vinegar; and balsamic vinegar. But in the spirit of working with what you've got, to make a proper substitution, the main thing to try to match is the vinegar's acidity level. Red and white wine vinegars can be safely swapped for one another, and while apple cider vinegar is less acidic than wine and sherry vinegars, I often substitute sherry vinegar when I've run out of one or another. The world of vinegar is vast, and extremely variable from region to region. It can be made from pretty much any fermentable liquid—fruit juice, beers, wines, grain spirits, kombucha—and it's a lot of fun to explore and experiment. When seasoning with acid, one of my favorite flavoring tricks is using a combination of vinegar (aged acid) and citrus (fresh acid).

MILD, SMOKY, SEMI-DRIED CHILI: A mild, smoky chili is one of my favorite enhancing ingredients, and I always have either Syrian Aleppo, or Turkish Marash/Maras pepper flakes on hand. These chilies are botanically the same but with different names, and they have a mild heat and smoky flavor, and a prominent fruitiness that's hard to replicate with other dried chilies. It's incredibly distinctive. They're also characterized by their somewhat coarse grind and moist texture. It's one of my go-to seasonings, and I highly recommend seeking out a bottle. To achieve the smokiness, you can use smoked paprika instead, but the fruitiness will be lost—there unfortunately isn't a perfect substitute. Burlap & Barrel's Silk Chili, a variety of Marash pepper, is my favorite.

FENNEL SEEDS: The anise flavor of fennel and fennel seeds doesn't please everyone, but I love it. It brings distinction to savory dishes, and usually takes people a bit by surprise. I like to add fennel seeds to marinades, salt blends, tisanes and other infusions, and soups, and they're also great added to granola and as a topping for crackers. I find that a high-quality one makes a big difference, and my favorite purveyor is Daphnis and Chloe.

OTHER DRIED SPICES: Mail-order options for dried spices are so abundant and exciting—much more so than the grocery store. My favorite spice purveyor is Burlap & Barrel (burlapandbarrel.com), which has a broad range of ethically and sustainably sourced spices from all over the globe. The Spice House (thespicehouse.com) is another terrific resource, as well as Frontier Co-Op (frontiercoop.com), which also distributes nationally. For spices that I know I won't use too often, I go to health and natural foods stores that sell them in bulk, where you can buy just a tablespoon or so, or however much you need.

FLOUR: Flour, given that it's made from a plant, goes rancid just like any other natural food, and is best purchased in quantities that you know you'll cycle through within a month or so. All-purpose flour can keep for a bit longer in an airtight container stored away from the sun, but less-processed specialty flours, which have a higher oil content because they contain the bran and germs of the grain, are actually quite delicate. Ideally, you should store these types of flours in the refrigerator or freezer.

I love incorporating whole-grain flours—whole wheat, barley, oat flour, spelt, among others—into my baking, primarily for flavor more than anything else, as they often deepen the wheaty flavors of a dish or add textural variety.

But they don't really behave the same way as all-purpose flour; they're hearty and usually "thirstier," meaning that they drink up the liquid in a dough or batter more aggressively than all-purpose flour does. If you wish to incorporate whole-grain flours into any of these recipes that don't call for them, I recommend substituting 25–30 percent of it in the all-purpose flour, going by weight rather than volume, which will contribute flavor and texture but not throw off the structural workings of the all-purpose flour.

I've also learned from many bakers that grocery-store whole-wheat flour isn't all that more special than all-purpose—in fact, it can even be regular all-purpose flour with wheat bran stirred back in. For flours that are fresh with flavor and that are true to the "whole-grain" ethos, seek out those marked "stone-ground." Hayden Flour Mills, Anson Mills, and Bob's Red Mill are all good resources.

A Note on Measuring Flour: Flour is notoriously difficult to measure reliably when done by volume. Every cook has a slightly different way of doing it (scooping, spooning, pouring straight from the bag), and each method produces a different amount of flour—and not every brand of 1-cup measuring cup even produces the same weight. So, even when it's done consistently, the results can vary. In these recipes, flour is always spooned—and not packed into the measuring cup—then leveled off with a knife. One cup of all-purpose flour should measure about 130 grams. For recipes where it really matters to get the right results, I prioritize the weight (in grams, which allows greater specificity than ounce measurements). If you don't have a scale, just be sure to use the spoon-then-level method.

SALT: My everyday, all-purpose salt has always been Diamond Crystal kosher salt, but over the past few years, for reasons I don't understand, it's become more difficult to find. So I started interchangeably using Morton's and the Whole Foods brands of kosher salt in these recipes. With salt, it's a good idea to become more dexterous and adapt. The primary difference between the two major kosher salts, Morton's and Diamond Crystal, is salt density: Morton's (and the Whole Foods brand) are almost twice as dense as Diamond Crystal, meaning that the same volume will be twice as salty. With savory cooking, you can simply taste as you go. But with baking, double the quantity if you're using Diamond Crystal kosher salt in these recipes.

MAPLE SYRUP AND HONEY: I use these sweeteners in dressings, sauces, dips, and really all over the place in my cooking. I don't necessarily use them interchangeably—the flavors are very different, and honey is more intensely sweet than maple syrup—but I know that many vegans don't eat honey, and often substitute maple syrup in its place. Just keep in mind that maple syrup has more water in its composition and therefore can affect overall texture, mouthfeel-wise. I always buy pure, real maple syrup, and the darker it is, the more intensely flavored it'll likely be. And like honey, it has "terroir"—meaning that its flavor varies based on where it's produced, which I say to encourage you to taste and explore. In buying honey, I find raw, runny honey to be the most versatile, and love to source it as locally as possible (which often means the farmers' market). If your honey crystallizes and hardens up, you can always warm it briefly and it will liquefy again—honey has no expiration date, so there's no excuse to ever toss it.

NUTS AND SEEDS: Nuts are probably a big part of your diet if you follow vegan, vegetarian, or even a partly plant-based diet, and it took much longer than it should have for me to recognize them as quite a perishable food. Once you begin to recognize the taste of a rancid nut, you'll immediately have an eagle eye for it—it's sharp, it's unpleasant, and it lingers. So store your nuts in your refrigerator or freezer to prolong their freshness, and then be sure to buy them at places where you know there's good turnover. Bulk bins can be a good option as long as you know that they're refreshed frequently. I'm also a big fan of nuts.com for nuts, seeds, and dried fruit and vegetables—their products are always fresh and shipped immediately, and their organic options are vast.

YEAST: When baking with yeast, I have the best, most consistent results using Saf-Instant yeast. Unlike "active" yeast, it doesn't need to be dissolved in liquid and proofed first—you just mix it into the dry ingredients and then proceed with the recipe. It's available in one-pound, vacuum-sealed pouches through many online retailers. Transfer it to a mason jar or other airtight container and store in your refrigerator for at least a year (and usually longer).

VEGAN SUBSTITUTIONS: Where applicable, I've done my best to offer vegan alternatives in these recipes. If you're vegan, I'm sure you're adept at tweaking non-vegan recipes. But for those that are new to their vegan journey, here are a few guidelines: When cheese or other dairy functions as a garnish-type component, such as in a salad, simply leave it out. If butter is called for in searing and sautéing applications, substitute a plant-based butter (Miyoko's Cultured Vegan Butter is my favorite) or oil. For quick breads and pancakes, my favorite egg substitute is a flax egg. When an egg white is called for, 2 tablespoons of aquafaba (the liquid in the can with chickpeas), whipped to soft peaks, works wonders.

THE THOUGHTFULLY THOUGHT-THROUGH SNACKY BITE

For me, preparing food for eating out of hand, which is how many of these recipes are meant to be eaten, means thinking through the experience in advance. I start by asking myself a number of questions: What's the right size for one bite? If it's a two-bite affair, will it hold together after biting it in half, or threaten to crumble all over my lap? How can it be composed so as to minimize drips, spills, or structural collapse? How can it be presented so that the whole system of eating it—such as pairing it with various other elements of the meal—feels intuitive? Will it leave hands sticky or oily?

In How to Crudités (page 107), I delve more deeply into how to present various cut-up vegetables to be dazzling to look at and also function well with dips and other elements of a snacky dinner, but much of the same logic applies to crackers and toasts. Aside from the flavors being complementary, is your cracker the right match given the consistency of your dip? Is it thick and dense? If so, you'll need a sturdy cracker that'll stand up to being dragged through. Or is it more thin and runny? Perhaps rather than a cracker, a more delicate vegetable like a blanched asparagus spear or green bean will be better, as it will easily coat the vegetable and feel more in proportion that way.

It's not my intention that you *over*think any of this, but I do find that spending a few moments to consider these factors can go a long way in making your snacks-for-dinner companions feel cared for—and this applies even when you're cooking just for yourself.

That said, it's always a good idea to keep cocktail napkins handy. Just in case.

KEY | Throughout the book, a ● next to a recipe means that it's particularly well suited for making ahead.

CRISPY-CRUNCHY | SAVORY, SNACKY BITES

Crispy, crunchy texture plays an essential role in any dish or meal, most importantly as a point of contrast against all the other non-crisp, non-crunchy textures. Even in the composition of a single *bite*, the same idea applies: think of a golden-crisp crouton in a bowl of velvety soup, or fragrant toasted nuts sprinkled over a salad of tender leaves, or the crunch of a tortilla chip against rich, creamy guacamole. Rarely is that burst of crunch the star attraction, but its supporting role is crucial to making the full experience an enjoyable one. And in a snacks-for-dinner meal, that's exactly the case.

These crispy-crunchy snack bites made of nuts, grains, and veggies can certainly stand alone, but in the composition of a snacky dinner, it can be helpful to think of them as garnishes for the whole meal. Here you'll find little handfuls of fragrant fried nuts or spicy snack mix; light-as-air "chips" made from Brussels sprouts leaves; and well-crisped parsnip fries that beg to be dragged through a spicy and tangy dip. They help break up some of the other bites—that wedge of a creamy cheese tart, or spoonful of soup—and also bring a little excitement.

In this chapter you'll find a treatise on stovetop popcorn—plus new ways to season it—and with a lifetime love of Chex party mix, I'm delighted to now share my own updated version, made extra savory with coconut oil, soy sauce, and crispy ramen noodles. Each recipe here promises a snap of some sort, and while these nibbles don't look like much, they have the potential to be the most memorable parts of your meal.

Beyond Snacks for Dinner

Crispy-crunchy epitomizes the word "snack" more than any other food trait. For that reason, let these be your *snack*-snacks as well, packing them with you for road trips, swim meets, hiking adventures, and more. The more fleetingly crispy-crunchy items, like Baked Brussels Sprouts Chips, the crispy Lemony Fried Chickpeas, and Lentil Snacking Granola, also function as inventive toppings for soups and salads.

CRISPY PARSNIP FRIES WITH GREEN CHILI + SUNFLOWER SEED ROMESCO

I love parsnips in all forms, but I especially love them as fries. Their floral flavor comes through and they take on a delicious caramelized crispiness if you cook them right. They have none of the cottony quality that can happen with oven-baked potato fries. I've found that they take quite a bit longer to cook than what you might expect—and without deep caramelization, they just won't be as good. Give them time to develop plenty of color, during which their texture also becomes appealingly tender. Use your senses as a guide more than the clock, and taste as you go. Like cabbage and leeks, they're a cold-weather crop, meaning that they benefit from being in the ground when the temperature drops to freezing—this crystallizes their sugars and makes them sweeter. So look for the best parsnips at farmers' markets in the late fall and through the winter.

Serves 4

2 pounds parsnips (about 6 medium or 4 large)
¼ cup olive oil

Kosher salt, to taste
Green Chili + Sunflower Seed Romesco (recipe below)

Preheat the oven to 400°F.

Trim the stem ends off the parsnips, then peel. Cut each one in half widthwise, and then in half lengthwise. Trim out the parsnip cores, which are too fibrous to enjoy as fries, and save them for stock or compost. Cut all the parsnip pieces into French-fry sizes, a little less than ¼ inch thick.

Place them in a mixing bowl with the olive oil, and sprinkle liberally with salt. Toss well. (It's better to use the mixing bowl than to do it on the baking sheet, as you want the parsnip pieces thoroughly coated in the oil.)

Spread them out on the baking sheet (using a spatula to include all the oil in the bowl as well) and transfer to the oven. Roast for 35 to 50 minutes, stirring every 15 minutes, until browned and crispy. Serve warm.

Green Chili + Sunflower Seed Romesco | Makes about 1 cup

This magical little dip highlights the nutty, vegetal flavor of sunflower seeds and presents it in a creamy format. Canned mild green chilies such as those made by Ortega, Old El Paso, or La Preferida, or even canned New Mexican hatch chilies (just be sure the can says "mild"), bring a little heat and also some tang. As a dip, it pairs terrifically with the parsnip fries, the Squash-Sunflower Sliders (page 142), and pretty much any other kind of chip or vegetable you happen to have nearby.

¼ cup raw sunflower seeds

One 4-ounce can mild green chilies

1 clove garlic, smashed

½ teaspoon kosher salt, and additional to taste

2 tablespoons olive oil

Juice of ½ lemon

Freshly ground black pepper

Spread the sunflower seeds out in a dry skillet, then toast over medium heat until fragrant and lightly browned, swirling the pan often, about 4 to 6 minutes. Allow to cool.

Combine the sunflower seeds with the green chilies, garlic, and salt in a food processor or mini food processor. Pulse to grind the nuts, scraping the sides as needed, then with the motor running add the oil and continue to process until pale and somewhat creamy. Add the lemon juice, pepper, and additional salt to taste.

LENTIL SNACKING GRANOLA

Equal parts cooked lentils and nuts and/or seeds provide all the body in this grain-free, savory granola, so it ends up being quite hearty (though by no means heavy). Egg white is the secret to its achieving sizable clumps, binding the nuts and lentils together into clusters. I like to keep these pieces larger because it makes the granola easier to snatch off a snack plate and eat out of hand, but of course you can break it up into smaller bits for sprinkling over yogurt or garnishing a soup. The yield works best on what restaurants call a "quarter sheet" pan, which is half the size of a regular baking sheet (see page 11). A small baking sheet or 9-by-13-inch dish works fine, too. For a standard baking sheet, it's best to double the recipe—otherwise the larger size forces it to spread out too much.

Makes 2 cups

1 egg white, or 2 tablespoons aquafaba
1 tablespoon olive oil
2 teaspoons sugar, brown or white
¾ teaspoon kosher salt
½ teaspoon dried thyme
½ teaspoon cumin seeds
¼ teaspoon mild smoky dried chili
   (Aleppo or Marash, see page 22), or a
   pinch of red pepper flakes

⅛ teaspoon ground black pepper
1 cup cooked lentils, cooled
1 cup mixed nuts and/or seeds
   (almonds, pecans, walnuts, hazelnuts,
   sesame seeds, sunflower seeds)

Preheat the oven to 325°F, and line a small (quarter) baking sheet or 9-by-13-inch baking dish with parchment paper. If using whole nuts, such as almonds, walnuts, or pecans, coarsely chop them.

If using egg white, whisk it with the oil, sugar, salt, thyme, and all the spices in the mixing bowl until it's broken down and the mixture appears a bit frothy. If using aquafaba, place it in a mixing bowl and beat until soft peaks form and the mixture becomes opaque, then stir in the oil, sugar, salt, thyme, and spices. Add the lentils and the nuts and/or seeds and stir well to coat evenly. Spread the mixture out on the prepared pan, and bake for 40 to 50 minutes, until the mixture is dry and the lentils crisp. Stir every 15 to 20 minutes, but aim to leave some of the clumps intact. Allow the mixture to cool, then store in an airtight container for up to a week. The mixture does lose a bit of its snap as it sits, but that never stops me from eating it.

SRIRACHA SNACK MIX WITH PUFFED RICE + PEANUTS

This addictive snack mix has it all: it's spicy, sweet, savory, and covers a whole spectrum of crunch. It never lasts long when I make it. The puffed rice from the breakfast cereal aisle is what gives it most of its body, but the world of store-bought puffed grains is ever expanding, and I encourage you to experiment. There are great options made from brown rice, quinoa, buckwheat, millet, and amaranth, and they're all healthfully made—a single ingredient! Just aim for something that's roughly the same size as puffed rice. And while you're cooking it, resist the urge to stir the pan too vigorously or too often, else the mixture won't end up having nice clusters.

Makes about 4 cups

2 tablespoons sriracha
2 tablespoons brown sugar
1 tablespoon apple cider vinegar
½ teaspoon kosher salt
¼ teaspoon ground black pepper
1 tablespoon maple syrup
1 cup unsalted peanuts
1 cup raw almonds
2 cups puffed rice

Preheat the oven to 325°F. Line a baking sheet with parchment paper.

In a mixing bowl, whisk together the sriracha, brown sugar, vinegar, salt, pepper, and maple syrup. Fold in the nuts and puffed rice, then spread out over a baking sheet. Transfer to the oven and bake, watching carefully toward the end, until the mixture darkens a shade, 25 to 30 minutes, stirring carefully just once. *Almost* burnt is the holy grail here, but if the mix does burn it can't be rescued.

Cool completely, then break the large pieces into bite-sized clumps. Store in an airtight container for up to 5 days.

Crispy-Crunchy | Savory, Snacky Bites

CHEX SNACK MIX REVISITED

Besides Whitney Houston's rendition of the national anthem, there are few things that stand out from the Super Bowl parties I attended growing up beyond the Chex party mix. It's a classic for a reason, and for me the best part is the Chex cereal, all crispy, buttery, and savory—the bagel and rye chips and other little crackers always felt a little superfluous. Here in my revisit of the recipe, I've created an assortment tailor-made to what I think is all the best stuff: nuts, seeds, Chex cereal—and the addition of crispy ramen noodles! For the spicing I've found a savory-sweet combination that's as addictive as the original, but know that the recipe is inherently flexible. You could swap butter or ghee for the coconut oil, and experiment with any spice blends you might have on hand—curry and masala blends would be excellent; just taste as you go to get the heat level right.

One note about the ramen: It's essential to get the instant noodles here, as they've been precooked and then fried (this is why they cook so quickly). Regular (uncooked, dried) wheat noodles that resemble the instant ramen ones (sometimes labeled "Chinese wheat noodles") won't get the same crisp, but more importantly, they'll soak up all the seasoning and create a bland, dry party mix that'll have you pleading for a glass of water.

Makes about 7 cups

3 tablespoons coconut oil

2 tablespoons soy sauce or tamari

2 tablespoons maple syrup

1 tablespoon brown sugar

1½ teaspoons mild smoky dried chili (Aleppo or Marash, see page 22)

3 ounces (1 pouch) instant ramen noodles, seasoning packet discarded

3 cups Chex cereal, any variety

2 cups unsalted, whole, raw or roasted mixed nuts (cashews, almonds, pecans, walnuts)

¼ cup hulled sunflower seeds

2 tablespoons sesame seeds

½ teaspoon coarse or flaky salt

Preheat the oven to 275°F. Line a baking sheet with parchment paper.

In a small saucepan, combine the coconut oil, soy sauce, maple syrup, brown sugar, and chili, and place over medium heat until the coconut oil is melted. (If your coconut is already in a liquid state, simply whisk these ingredients together in a large mixing bowl and proceed with the next step.)

In a large mixing bowl, break up the ramen noodles into bite-sized pieces; try to keep them in little clusters rather than shattering them into shards. Add the cereal, nuts, and seeds and stir to combine, then pour the coconut oil mixture over and stir well to coat everything evenly.

Scrape the mixture onto the prepared baking sheet and spread into an even layer and sprinkle with the salt. Transfer to the oven and bake for 60 to 75 minutes, until the nuts are lightly browned and the mixture feels dry. It will crisp up further as it cools. Once cool, store in an airtight container.

Crispy-Crunchy | Savory, Snacky Bites

SMOKY GLAZED PISTACHIOS

This glazed nut treatment can be used for almonds, cashews, or walnuts, but I'm leading with pistachios because we included them with our wedding snack boxes (page 149), where they were the perfect, just-decadent-enough crunchy thing that rose to the occasion and rounded out the snacks we made for our guests. Ghee has such an impact here, giving the nuts deeply fragrant and buttery—for lack of a better word—*nuttiness*. It shocks me every time, how such little bit goes such a long way. Roasting any nuts in a bit of ghee infuses them with flavor, and hopefully this inspires you to experiment with ghee in your other roasting and toasting, but the honey and smoked chili transform nuts into a next-level treat. Know that the nuts will still seem a bit wet when they come out of the oven, but the glaze hardens as the nuts cool and take on a candied appearance. And as with all candying and glazing cooking, humidity is not your friend—the honey just won't fully harden because of all the moisture in the air—so I don't recommend making these on a sweaty summer day.

Makes 1 cup

2 teaspoons ghee, clarified butter, or butter	1 teaspoon mild, smoky, dried chili (Aleppo or Marash, see page 22)
1 tablespoon honey	½ teaspoon kosher salt
1 cup raw, shelled pistachios	

Preheat the oven to 325°F.

In a medium, oven-safe skillet, warm the ghee over medium-low heat. Add the honey, swirling the pan over the heat until the honey becomes a bit runny, then stir in the pistachios, coating them well, and sprinkle with the chili and salt.

Transfer to the oven and cook, stirring every 10 minutes, until the coating thickens significantly and the nuts have darkened a shade, about 25 to 30 minutes. They'll still look a bit wet, but as they cool, the coating will harden. Scrape them onto a plate right after you take them from the oven and allow to cool completely.

Feta + Jam Tart (p. 117)

Smoky Glazed Pistachios (p. 40)

STOVETOP POPCORN + FUN WAYS TO SERVE IT

Not everybody thinks to put popcorn on the dinner table, but it's actually a perfect blank canvas as far as crispy-crunchy items go, and it can be seasoned in any number of ways to make it complement the rest of a snacks-for-dinner meal. Below are three fun directions for seasoning, and I also encourage you to dig up any seasoning blends you have lingering around, or try the Herby Seasoning Blends on page 123. My instructions for stovetop popcorn might seem fussy, but the fact is, most of the stovetop popcorn I've made over the years has been hugely frustrating. So often I'd get either burnt, acrid popcorn, or only half-popped kernels, no matter how foolproof the method I was following promised to be. Thankfully, I figured out where I was going wrong: First, a thinner pot works better than a heavy-bottomed one. Second, adjust the heat as you go; unless you're using an induction burner, your pot is going to continue to build heat despite the output staying the same, so plan to turn down the heat a touch once the kernels start popping. Third, the popping comes in waves! It's more important to listen for rattling of unpopped kernels inside the pot than it is to count seconds between pops.

Makes 7 to 8 cups, enough to serve 4

2 tablespoons high-smoke-point oil, such as grapeseed or avocado oil	½ cup popcorn kernels Seasoning of choice (see below)

Measure your popcorn and set it aside, and place a pot, one that comes with a lid, over medium heat. Add the oil to the pot and 3 to 5 of the popcorn kernels. Cover the pot and listen for them to start popping. Once you've heard each one pop, pour in the rest of the kernels and immediately cover. Swirl the pan to coat them all in oil, and leave undisturbed on the heat until you begin to hear popping. Once you do, every 30 to 60 seconds swirl or gently shake the pot while holding the lid in place, using mitted hands, which will keep the unpopped kernels settling down on the bottom, closest to the heat. Continue swirling until the popping subsides. It may be helpful to tinker with the heat, raising it in the beginning if the kernels seem slow to pop, and then lowering it toward the end to prevent burning. Additionally, I often find that there's a second, and sometimes a third, wave of popping between quiet stretches, so listen carefully as you swirl for the sound of unpopped kernels, shaking the pot often. Try not to open the lid, which will allow all the heat trapped inside to escape. Once 5 to 8 seconds pass between a few lone pops and the sound of unpopped kernels rattling around inside grows fainter, turn off the heat and transfer the popped corn to a large bowl, reserving the pot for preparing the seasonings.

(cont.)

Crispy-Crunchy | Savory, Snacky Bites

Nutritional Yeast + Olive Oil + Smoky Chili

2 tablespoons olive oil
1½ tablespoons nutritional yeast

1½ teaspoons smoky dried chili, such as
   Aleppo or Marash (see page 22)
¾ to 1 teaspoon kosher salt
Freshly ground black pepper

Once the pot used for popping has cooled for about 2 minutes, add the olive oil to the pan, then the popcorn, and toss to coat. Sprinkle the nutritional yeast, chili, salt, and pepper, and toss to combine.

Coconut Oil + Garam Masala + Pinch of Sugar

3 tablespoons coconut oil
2 teaspoons garam masala

1 teaspoon sugar
¾ to 1 teaspoon kosher salt

Once the pot used for popping has cooled for about 2 minutes, add the coconut oil, swirling until it's melted (you may need to apply low or medium heat). Stir in the garam masala and sugar until fragrant, then the popcorn, tossing to coat. Toss with the salt and taste, adding more salt as needed.

Freeze-Dried Raspberries + Coconut Oil

½ cup freeze-dried raspberries
3 tablespoons coconut oil
1 teaspoon ground sumac (optional)

½ teaspoon sugar
½ to ¾ teaspoons kosher salt

In a mortar and pestle, grind the raspberries to a fine powder (alternatively, place them in a resealable bag and run over them a few times with a rolling pin).

Once the pot used for popping has cooled for about 2 minutes, add the coconut oil to the pan, swirling until it's melted (you may need to apply low or medium heat). Add the popcorn and toss to combine, followed by the raspberry powder, sumac if using, sugar, and salt. Taste, adding more salt as needed.

BAKED BRUSSELS SPROUTS CHIPS

You want these Brussels salty and crisp, like potato chips. To maximize crispiness, you'll need to spend a few minutes separating the leaves from the cores, and this works best when you buy the more mature, large Brussels sprouts that sometimes can appear already unfurled a bit, rather than the young, tight buds. And you'll have cores and root trimmings leftover, which can be put to use in the limey sauté that follows the recipe, or in the Brussels Sprouts with Peanuts + Yuba (page 162), which will be exactly the right volume you need for that recipe. Serve these simply with a liberal sprinkling of flaky salt, or give them some personality with any type of seasoning. If you plan to season them after baking, take care to not oversalt the leaves before putting them in the oven.

Makes about 3 cups

1 pound large Brussels sprouts	Flaky salt
2 tablespoons melted coconut oil	

Preheat the oven to 450°F.

Separate the outer leaves of the Brussels sprouts from the cores by trimming a sliver of the root end of each one off, so that an outer layer of leaves can be gently tugged off. Repeat this process, going as far as you can until you get to the tight core, where leaves can't easily be separated anymore. Be a bit persistent trying to dislodge as many leaves as you can—more leaves, more chips! Reserve the cores for the sauté recipe below.

In a mixing bowl, use your hands to toss the leaves with the coconut oil, coating them evenly and well. Divide between two baking sheets, taking care to separate each leaf so that none are clinging (or spooning) one another—they won't cook evenly if they're stuck together. Sprinkle with a few pinches of salt, knowing that the leaves will shrink a bit in the oven and the saltiness will concentrate.

Bake for 10 minutes, then reduce the temp to 350 and bake for about 5 to 10 minutes more, until well browned and completely crisp. As you stir, take care to keep the leaves separated— again, any that are stuck together will steam and take longer to get crispy.

Allow to cool before serving. These are best eaten within a few hours of baking.

Sauté of Sprouts Cores: Slice the remaining Brussels sprouts cores into thin rounds or quarters, and combine them with the root-end trimmings. Warm a tablespoon of oil in a medium skillet, over medium heat. Add the sprouts and cook until they soften slightly and begin to caramelize in parts, shaking or stirring periodically, 6 to 8 minutes. Remove from the heat and stir in the zest of 1 lime, half of its juice, a few pinches of salt, and freshly ground black pepper to taste. Add additional salt and lime juice as needed. Serve warm or at room temperature.

BEER CHEESE GOUGERES

Gougeres, aka cheese puffs, have the power to signal to anyone present that, yes, what's happening right now is a party. They make for a perfect little bite that's crispy, gooey, cheesy, and somehow practically weightless. But they're also easy to make in advance so that you can bake off just a few for a Tuesday night snacky dinner if that's your kind of thing. Just portion out the dough, freeze them, and then keep them in an airtight container—they can be baked straight out of the freezer. In this recipe, I took the classic formula and infused it with the flavor of Kentucky beer cheese—which is a delicious spread made from sharp cheddar cheese and beer—plus a few spices that play up the malty, bitter, cheesy flavors. I recommend a strong brown ale here, otherwise the beer flavor will be too subtle.

Makes about 2 dozen

1 cup brown ale
1 stick (4 ounces) butter
1/2 teaspoon kosher salt
1 cup all-purpose flour
2 teaspoons dry mustard
1/2 teaspoon ground black pepper

1/4 teaspoon ground cayenne pepper
4 eggs
1 teaspoon vegan Worcestershire sauce
4 ounces (about 1 1/2 cups) grated sharp
    cheddar cheese

Preheat the oven to 425°F. Line 2 baking sheets with parchment paper. If you have time, pour the beer into a glass and let stand for 20 to 30 minutes so that it loses some of its carbonation.

Combine the beer, butter, and salt in a medium saucepan and bring to a boil. Add the flour, mustard, black pepper, and cayenne all at once and stir vigorously, using a wooden spoon, until a smooth dough forms and a light doughy film appears over the bottom of the pan. Continue stirring for about 2 minutes more to fully cook the flour and dry out the dough, then remove from the heat and let stand for 5 minutes to cool.

You'll need to beat the eggs into the dough, which requires some elbow grease if you do it by hand with a wooden spoon. You can absolutely use a hand mixer or stand mixer fitted with the paddle attachment instead. In either case, add eggs one by one, beating well after each addition, followed by the Worcestershire sauce. With each egg, the mixture will look like it's breaking into big, slimy curds, but rest assured the dough will come together as you mix. Last, beat in the cheese.

Arrange neat scoops about 2 tablespoons of batter each over the prepared baking sheets, spacing them at least an inch apart. (A spring-loaded ice cream/cookie dough scoop, 2 tablespoons in volume, is perfect for this.) Transfer to the oven and bake for 22 to 26 minutes, until puffed and golden brown, and evenly browned on the bottoms as well. Serve immediately.

LEMONY FRIED CHICKPEAS

As you'll see in the handful of fried recipes in this book, I'm a big fan of shallow-frying. The method is simply the opposite of deep-frying: rather than filling up a pan with enough oil to submerge whatever you're cooking in it, you'll use only enough to partially submerge the food. Be diligent in flipping and moving it to ensure that it cooks evenly—it's a great way to not waste so much oil, but still get crispy-golden crusts. I use that method here, because while I've attempted many different recipes for crispy chickpeas that use the oven over the years, none of them are as good as fried ones. I especially like them with a pronounced lemony tang, which is achieved by soaking the beans in lemon juice and then dousing them in lemon zest right after they come out of the pan. Unfortunately, they lose their crispy coating relatively quickly, so it's best to make these within an hour or two of when you want to eat them.

Makes about 3 cups

2 lemons	Olive oil, for frying
Two 14.5-ounce cans, or 3½ cups homecooked, chickpeas	Kosher salt, to taste
	A few pinches dried oregano

Using a rasp-style grater, zest the lemons, and set the zest aside.

Drain the chickpeas (reserving the aquafaba if you have a use for it) and rinse them well, and drain again. Spread out on a clean towel and blot dry, then transfer to a mixing bowl and add the juice of the lemons. Let stand for 20 to 30 minutes.

Using a spider skimmer or slotted spoon, lift the chickpeas out of the lemon juice and return to the clean towel and gently but thoroughly blot dry one last time. (The lemon juice can be used for a vinaigrette or marinade.)

In your widest skillet, add enough oil to measure ¼ inch deep, and place over medium-high heat. If you use a medium-sized, 10-inch skillet, you'll need to fry the chickpeas in batches—it's important that the chickpeas fit in a single layer where they're not too crammed together. Once the oil is hot (test the temperature by adding a single chickpea; it should sizzle immediately), add as many chickpeas as will fit in a single layer and fry until golden brown all over and crispy, about 15 minutes, swirling and stirring the pan periodically. The mixture may get foamy as it cooks, which is normal—just lift a few chickpeas out of the pan to check on doneness. When golden, transfer them to a paper towel-lined plate or baking sheet using a slotted spoon. (If cooking the chickpeas in batches, add more oil to the pan with each new batch.)

Immediately sprinkle the chickpeas liberally with salt, then add the lemon zest and a few pinches of dried oregano. Serve warm or immediately after they've cooled—ideally within an hour, as they soften and lose their crispiness relatively quickly.

CRISPY BROILED MAITAKE MUSHROOMS

These broiled mushrooms get delicately crisp at the feathery ends, but stay succulent toward the stems, and while they're an unexpected riff on a chip, they're a total delight to snack on. This is a very simple cooking method that allows for careful supervision, because I know maitake mushrooms (also called hen-of-the-woods mushrooms) can be a bit of a splurge. Where I live, they're in season in the fall. Use good olive oil and balsamic vinegar that has some nuance, the latter of which even adds a bit of a candied crust. When shopping for the mushrooms, try to buy one or two large pieces—their base ends tend to dry and harden up quickly and need to be trimmed off, and the more mushroom pieces you start with, the more trimmings there will be. (Save those trimmings for stock, though.) Try to cook them off within a day or two of purchasing them, to prevent any further drying out.

Serves 4

Neutral-tasting, high-smoke-point oil, such as grapeseed or avocado oil
1½ pounds maitake mushrooms (also known as hen-of-the-woods mushrooms)

2 teaspoons good balsamic vinegar
About 1 teaspoon fresh lemon juice
Good olive oil
Flaky salt
Freshly ground black pepper

Preheat the broiler to high. Rub about 2 teaspoons of the neutral-tasting oil over a baking sheet.

Working gently so as to have minimal mushroom debris, break the large mushrooms into smaller clusters—think of them as two- or three-bite morsels—and arrange them in a single layer on the baking sheet. Drizzle lightly with additional neutral-tasting oil, and then, using your hands, very gently toss to distribute the oil more evenly.

Place the pan directly beneath the heat source and broil for 7 minutes, rotating the pan once, until they begin to char and crispen, but are still a bit raw toward the stems. If a good deal of liquid has collected in the pan, cook for another 2 to 5 minutes, until it cooks off and the mushrooms are visibly taking on some color and crisping up. Sprinkle with 2 teaspoons of balsamic vinegar, then return to the broiler and cook for 1 to 3 minutes more, until evenly crisp and just tender in their thicker parts.

You can serve these hot or at room temperature. Just before serving, drizzle with olive oil, a few spritzes of lemon juice, and sprinkle liberally with coarse salt and freshly ground black pepper.

GENTLY FRIED NUTS WITH ROSEMARY

Every Christmas, my grandma would take me with her to Lee's Candies in Boise, Idaho, to pick up our family's annual 2-pound box of milk-chocolate-covered mint creams (they're the absolute best, should you be lucky enough to get your hands on them) and a bag or two of their fried cashews, which she'd add to the appetizer and cookie assortments over the holiday festivities. Packed tightly into cellophane bags, they are locked in my mind as the ideal version of a cashew: golden-brown as if sun-soaked, and flecked with salt crystals that'd catch the light in the shop. It's remarkable that cashews have become so common in my diet when, at that time, it was inconceivable to think of them as anything but an incredible delicacy. While those nuts are definitely deep- rather than shallow-fried, I have wonderful results using less oil when I recreate them, and also in using olive oil, which is more flavorful. The trick is to pay close attention to the heat. If it's too low, the nuts will simply absorb the oil and take forever to fry, but if it's too hot, then the outsides will burn before the nuts are toasted all the way through. Be attentive as you fry them, to maintain some steady, gentle sizzling.

Makes 2 cups

½ cup olive oil
2 cups raw cashews or almonds

¼ cup rosemary leaves (from about 2 long sprigs)
Flaky salt, to taste

In a medium skillet, such as a cast-iron one, warm the oil over medium-low heat. Add one nut to check the temperature—it should sizzle gently. If sizzling is aggressive, turn down the heat, and if there's no activity, remove the nut and wait another minute. When it's ready, add the rest of the nuts. Stir often, watching closely, reducing the heat if they start to color too quickly or burn. Over the course of 10 to 15 minutes, the cashews will turn a warm golden-brown and the almonds will darken a shade (you can test doneness by cutting a nut in half—it should be browned all the way through) and become very fragrant. Stir in the rosemary leaves, which will cause the oil to sizzle a bit. Cook for 1 to 3 minutes more to allow the rosemary to crispen, then use a slotted spoon to transfer the nuts and rosemary to a paper towel-lined plate. Immediately sprinkle with salt. Allow to cool for at least 10 minutes, which will give the nuts time to get crunchy again. Serve warm or at room temperature. These are most delicious while still warm, but once cool, store them in an airtight container. They'll keep for about a week.

Crispy-Crunchy | Savory, Snacky Bites

Three Tips for Upping Your Knife Game

Due to the fact that so much produce is involved, vegetarian and vegan cooking inherently means more slicing and dicing. And I can't emphasize enough what a difference it makes to build your confidence with a knife so that you can slice and dice quickly and safely. I always recommend that people take a knife skills class (there are now many available online), but in the interest of not overwhelming you, I want to focus here on just three core principles, designed specifically for using an 8-to-10-inch chef's knife—which can be a workhorse in your kitchen if you know how to use it.

THE PINCH GRIP: While it's called the "handle," your knife handle alone is not actually sufficient for holding it properly. Rather, by choking up on the handle, such that your thumb and index finger are gripping the blade—the area of the knife known as the bolster—you'll have much greater control. In knife school lingo, this is called the "pinch grip."

It moves the fulcrum of the knife (your hand) to its center, rather than at the handle, and it limits your wrist mobility. The result is a sturdier grip that moves more steadily as you work.

When you're working with a large piece of food, the pinch grip also helps anchor the tip of the knife on your cutting board, making a rocking back-and-forth motion feel natural, as the blade is steady and you are in control of its motions.

THE CLAW: As for your other hand, there's a safe and steady way to hold the food that you're cutting, referred to as "the claw" grip. The principle here is, first, don't splay any of your fingers out on the cutting board, making them vulnerable to a moving, very sharp object. Rather, hold your wrist upright over the food you're cutting as if gripping a tennis ball, with your fingertips tucked under, following the curve of the imaginary ball. Additionally, this turns your knuckle into a guide for uniform cuts, as it is propped up at 90 degrees from the board. This can be especially useful for making thin slices.

THE PRINCIPLE OF FLAT SURFACES: The last step, which may seem obvious, is what I call the "principle of flat surfaces." Very few produce items lie flat on the cutting board, and in fact, most of them are inclined to roll around. Before doing anything else, the first thing I do to a piece of produce, whether it's an onion, a carrot, or a butternut squash, is make a cut that forces it to lie flat—and thus stay put.

Once it's flat, prepping it becomes a matter of how to strategize efficient cuts. For example, think of it as a process of making "planks," or other long, wide slabs; they can then be stacked on top of one another and cut into strips; and after that, you can group the strips and cut them into squares. Not every vegetable lends itself to being perfectly diced into squares, but the principle is almost always the

same—trimming large pieces into more manageable, similarly sized pieces, then grouping them to trim them down further.

A FINAL NOTE: Keep your knives sharp by honing them once a week or so. This process of running the knife down a long metal or ceramic rod straightens its cutting edge, but it will make it feel sharper and help it make smoother cuts. Then have it professionally sharpened, or learn how to sharpen them at home, which will only need to be done once or twice a year depending on how much cooking you do.

TANGY-JUICY | PICKLES + MARINADES

A pickle might seem optional, more of a diner or deli type of thing than a necessary part of a home-cooked meal. That'd always been my perspective, anyway, particularly as someone with limited appetite for strongly acidic and tangy condiments (vegetarian and vegan dishes just don't always have the force of meat's flavor to counterbalance a puckery hit of acid). But a few discoveries have shifted my thinking, the first being quick pickles. Quick-pickling as a method sidesteps all the questions about canning and pH and whatnot, and you can think of them instead simply as seasoned vegetables that are dressed with vinegar and stored in the fridge for a week or so. "Pickling" them this way extends their shelf life (though not nearly as long as traditional canning methods), but what I like best about the quick-pickling is that it preserves the freshness of the vegetable in its raw state.

The other shift in my thinking happened from understanding that "pickle" means something different to practically every cuisine, ranging from kosher dills and sugary pickled watermelon rind, to Korean kimchi, Moroccon preserved lemons, and South Indian achars, which can be oil-based. The recipes in this chapter thus take a liberal approach to the pickle category, aiming to accommodate on-the-fly cooking and to offer resourceful ways to make use of smaller amounts of vegetables with quick-pickling methods only. And I've grouped them with what I'm calling "marinades," which means here that you'll pair a vegetable with a zingy, oil-based marinade and let it sit for an hour or a few days to become more flavorful over time.

The Spicy Zucchini Quick Pickles are the perfect answer to a summertime zucchini glut, and the Gingery Quick-Pickled Beets have a little heat but also a savory kick, working perfectly as toppings for a soft cheese and a homemade cracker. And the "marinades" are probably my favorites, because they're secretly quite hearty. The Citrus Carrots could easily be called "cold carrot steaks," since they're a fork-and-knife job, and the Oyster Mushrooms in Walnut Oil are a decadent treat. Beyond bringing some color and fresh, juicy textures that contrast so well with other foods, these methods serve to capture the fleeting freshness of a few vegetables, prolonging them a little longer.

Beyond Snacks for Dinner

These pickled and marinated vegetables brighten up any meal once you've prepared them and packed them away in the refrigerator. Add them to grain bowls, salads, sandwiches, and skillet-scramble breakfasts. They can make bland dishes like, say, scrambled egg whites or low-fat cottage cheese taste interesting and exciting.

SPICY ZUCCHINI QUICK PICKLES

Zucchini has a nutty, sweet flavor, and it's remarkable how a quick toss with salt can make them addictive, seasoning them and drawing out enough water to make them pliable. These pickles are an easy way to transform them into a spicy condiment that'll enliven all manner of snacky bites. It's also a great place to experiment with fresh chilies, especially if your farmers' market offers a variety in late summer, as fresh chili offerings can be so inconsistent at grocery stores. Any hot chili would be great here, and I find that splitting it in half doesn't overwhelm the pickles with heat, but if you wish to be cautious, leave it whole. While the habanero *is* hot, the tingling heat it adds to these pickles doesn't set your mouth on fire so much as draw attention to its fruity, floral flavor.

Makes about 3 cups

12 to 14 ounces zucchini (2 small or 1 medium)	1 clove garlic
	3 black peppercorns
¾ teaspoon kosher salt	1 clove
1 habanero pepper, halved through the stem	⅔ cup white wine vinegar
	½ teaspoon sugar

Thinly slice the zucchini into rounds about ⅛ inch thick, ideally using a mandoline. Toss with the salt, then transfer to a colander or sieve and allow to drain for at least 30 minutes, and up to an hour. This will draw out water from the vegetable, so be sure to set it over a bowl or in the sink. After that time, the zucchini slices should be pliable and well seasoned. Give the vegetables a gentle squeeze to extract some additional liquid, then pack into 3- to 4-cup jar. Add the habanero, garlic, peppercorns, and clove.

In a tall measuring glass, whisk together the vinegar and sugar until the sugar dissolves. Pour this over the zucchini. Add additional water so the vegetables are just submerged. Seal and place in the refrigerator overnight. Stored in the jar, they'll keep for at least 2 weeks.

CITRUS CARROTS

These carrots have become a staple at my house because they're incredibly flavorful, but also feel "meaty" in a way that's got vegetable-charcuterie vibes. In the context of a snacking dinner they bring color and tang and complement a wide array of savory bites. I often don't peel organic carrots—I just give them a good scrub—and for this recipe I like to leave them in large quarters or halves (make sure to trim them into your desired pieces for serving before combining them with the marinade—once they're coated in the marinade they become slippery and difficult to cut). I set them out on a small plate so that diners can serve themselves, using them to build little toasts or enjoying them on their own.

Makes about 4 cups

1 pound carrots, trimmed and peeled	1 tablespoon lemon juice
Kosher salt	¼ teaspoon freshly ground black
¼ cup orange juice	pepper
¼ cup white wine vinegar	¼ cup olive oil

Slice or quarter the carrots lengthwise so that they're all roughly the same thickness, then cover with water in a medium saucepan. Bring to a boil, add 1 teaspoon salt, and cook until the carrots are just tender and have lost their crunch but are not yet mushy—8 to 12 minutes. Drain and cool. Taste the carrots. You want them well seasoned, and if they're not, add a few extra pinches of salt to the marinade.

Meanwhile, whisk together orange juice, vinegar, lemon juice, pepper, olive oil, and remaining ½ teaspoon salt in a shallow container, ideally one that comes with an airtight lid. Add the cooled carrots, seal the container, and store in the fridge overnight for the flavors to develop. Stored in the marinade, they'll keep for up to a week. Lift the carrots out of the marinade for serving.

Tangy Carrot Whip | Makes about 2 cups

Coarsely chop 1½ cups of chopped, marinated carrots, place them in a high-powered blender or food processor, and puree. Add 3 tablespoons well-stirred tahini and process once more to combine, then, with the motor running, pour in 2 tablespoons of the marinade. If you go the food processor route, let the motor run for several minutes to achieve the smoothest possible consistency. Taste for seasoning before serving.

Warm, Revived Olives (p. 74)

Mixed Mushroom Pâté (p. 82)

Citrus Carrots (p. 60)

HONEYED PICKLED SHALLOTS

A jar of quick-pickled shallots in the fridge is such a help to dress up simple foods like bowls of rice, steamed or roasted vegetables, brothy beans, scrambled eggs, and avocado toasts, and the same goes for a snacky dinner. They're an effortless pop of flavor for those bites that seem to be missing something. Honey gives the shallots a rounded sweetness, softening the acid and lending some fruity complexity to the pickle. I especially like to use them as a garnish for Orange + Mustard Marinated Asparagus (page 67), Mixed Mushroom Pâté (page 82), Dill + White Bean Spread (page 106), and Toasted Walnut + Feta Dip (page 83)—just set out a bowl of the pickled shallots and let people assemble their crackers and toasts as they please.

Makes about 1½ cups

6 medium-large shallots (8 to 10 ounces)	1 tablespoon honey
½ cup white wine vinegar	1 teaspoon kosher salt
½ cup water	3 black peppercorns

Trim off the tops of the shallots and, leaving them whole, pull off all the papery skin. Using a mandoline, or a steady hand and a sharp knife, cut them into thin rounds about ⅛ inch thick, almost to the root, then discard the roots.

In a small saucepan, bring the vinegar, water, honey, salt, and peppercorns to a simmer. Add the shallots and bring the mixture back to a simmer, which will take only a minute or two, and during which time the shallots should have softened and collapsed enough that they're mostly submerged by the liquid. They should still have a raw bite. Transfer the contents of the pan to a heatproof pint jar and allow to cool, then store, lidded, in the fridge for up to 2 weeks.

UMAMI ROASTED TOMATOES

There's nothing wrong with simple, slow-roasted tomatoes, but the addition of a bit of soy sauce offers some exciting complexity, doubling down on the umami nature of the fruit. You don't want to dry out the tomatoes completely—they should be concentrated in flavor, but still juicy—and to prevent the drying out from happening, it's best to roast them in a snug single layer, which can be a large oven-safe skillet, a quarter sheet pan, or a 9-by-13-inch baking dish. You could also use larger tomatoes if they're in season, as long as you adjust the cooking time accordingly. Serve these as a complement to still-warm Perfect Boiled Eggs (page 125), spooned over soft, fresh cheese like ricotta or Cultured Cashew Ricotta (page 89), or as a simple topping for toasts and crackers.

Makes about 2 cups

2 pints cherry tomatoes, halved (about 20 ounces by weight)

2 tablespoons olive oil

1 tablespoon dark soy sauce

¼ to ½ teaspoon kosher salt

Freshly ground black pepper

Preheat the oven to 280°F.

In a mixing bowl, combine the tomatoes with the oil, soy sauce, ¼ teaspoon salt, and a few grinds of black pepper. Spread them out, cut side up, on a baking sheet or vessel or in a pan in which they fit in a snug single layer, such as a quarter sheet pan, 9-by-13-inch baking dish, or large oven-safe skillet.

Transfer to the oven and bake until the tomatoes have shrunk a bit and are concentrated in flavor but still juicy, about 90 minutes, gently shaking the pan or stirring every 30 minutes. Taste along the way, adding additional pinches of salt as needed—since they concentrate in flavor, it can be easy to oversalt them before they go into the oven, which is why I like to salt as I go.

Once cooled, transfer the tomatoes and all the pan juices into an airtight container and store in the fridge, where they'll keep for a week.

GINGERY QUICK-PICKLED BEETS

These get more gingery over time, gaining noticeable heat and spice over the span of even just one day. Purple, yellow, or the striped chioggia beets (sometimes called the bull's-eye beet) all work, and you can cut them down into any shape you prefer—thin rounds are nice, as are cubes—but I like matchsticks best, which just work a little better when pairing customized bites with dips and cheese. The cooking time will vary depending on the size you choose. As always, taste as you go, cooking them long enough to mellow the raw bite while leaving a bit of crunch intact; I don't think they're nearly as good when totally soft. These add a little blast of color to any spread and a bright tanginess that complements crudité plates, soft cheese and savory pâtés with toasts and crackers, and boiled eggs, and once you've got them on hand, they add a great deal of distinction to sandwiches, grain bowls, and omelets, too.

Makes about 1 pint

1 medium-large beet (12 to 16 ounces)	½ cup water
3 black peppercorns	1 tablespoon sugar
2 allspice berries	1½ teaspoons kosher salt
1 clove	1 ounce ginger, scrubbed clean of any
½ cup apple cider vinegar or rice vinegar	debris and sliced into thin slabs

Bring a saucepan of water to boil. Meanwhile, peel the beet (using gloves if you wish to avoid staining your hands), and then cut into ¼-inch matchsticks, or any other shape you please. Lower the beet pieces into the water and par-cook until just tender enough that the raw bite is gone—I like a little bit of snap—usually 2 to 5 minutes, or more, depending on the size of your pieces.

Drain the beets, and then transfer them to a wide-mouthed 2-cup-capacity jar or container, and add the peppercorns, allspice berries, and clove.

Back in the saucepan, combine the vinegar, water, sugar, salt, and ginger and bring to a boil. Pour this over the beets, ensuring that they are submerged. If not, add equal parts vinegar and water as needed. Once cool, seal the jar and keep in the fridge. The flavors will be most developed after a day, and the beets will keep for at least 2 weeks.

ORANGE + MUSTARD MARINATED ASPARAGUS

I remember what a revelation it was to my mom when she learned to cook asparagus for just 4 minutes. (She'd set a timer—the 4 minutes was sacrosanct.) As a kid, she dreaded seeing them on her plate because they were always cooked to stringy, pale-green mush. But when *just* tender, and not at all mushy, and vibrantly green, it's such a pleasing, juicy vegetable. Cooked this way, it's always been one of my favorites. This method of marinating it is one I particularly like for super-fresh, springtime asparagus, but even in the off-season, it does wonders to make it interesting and delicious when it's not exactly at its peak. You'll cook it immediately, shock in cold water, then combine with this zesty marinade. The hot, sweet mustard gives the marinade distinction—I love it with my Stovetop Maple-Ale Mustard (page 100)—but you can use Dijon or any other hot or horseradish mustard if that's what you've got on hand.

Serves 4 to 6

1 pound asparagus spears	2 teaspoons fresh thyme leaves, or
1 orange	½ teaspoon dried
2 teaspoons sweet hot mustard, such as	¼ teaspoon kosher salt
Stovetop Maple-Ale Mustard	2 tablespoons olive oil
(page 100)	

Remove the woody ends of the asparagus by bending them in half and letting the ends snap off. Compost the tough ends or reserve them for another use. Wash the asparagus thoroughly by swishing them around in a bowl of water—grit can often be trapped in the tips and little petals along the sides. Set aside the asparagus, rinse out the bowl, and prepare an ice bath.

In a pot (or a saucepan that's wide enough for the asparagus to lie flat), add about ½ inch of water and bring to a simmer. Fit the pot with a steamer insert, then add the asparagus and cook until *just* tender—2 to 3 minutes for skinny spears, and 3 to 5 minutes for larger ones. Avoid overcooking them. Transfer to the ice bath to halt the cooking, then drain and blot dry with a kitchen towel.

To prepare the dressing, zest the orange and add to a mixing bowl, then squeeze in 2 tablespoons of its juice. Add the mustard, thyme leaves, and salt, and whisk to combine. Whisk in the oil in a steady stream. Add the asparagus, stir to coat, and then store in an airtight container in the fridge for up to 4 days.

OYSTER MUSHROOMS IN WALNUT OIL

A few years ago I had the good fortune of working with the wildly creative chef Lauren Gerrie on a photo shoot for *Jarry* magazine in which she translated a few iconic "looks" of her then-client Marc Jacobs into plated dishes. For a flowing, pale-pink dress from one of his collections, she created a dish made from a few big, meaty pieces of pink oyster mushrooms that had been pickled in walnut oil. It was an ingenious interpretation and also incredibly delicious. I haven't been able to forget what a beautiful pairing the delicate mushrooms and the nutty oil are, and used that as inspiration here, where the mushrooms are briefly cooked in walnut oil, as well as a bit of acid and some spices. This is a luxurious dish, and while it's just a marinated (or arguably pickled) vegetable, it has center-of-the-plate potential when the mushrooms are big, meaty, and fresh. It pairs well with all kinds of cheese and among other types of prepared vegetables and salads. Marjoram may be a harder-to-find herb, but it's well worth seeking out (or adding to your herb planter boxes) for its vibrant, slightly sweeter flavor than fresh oregano.

Makes about 2 cups

6 to 7 ounces fresh oyster mushrooms
½ cup walnut oil
2 tablespoons neutrally flavored oil,
  such as grapeseed or avocado oil
1 tablespoon sherry vinegar

¼ teaspoon kosher salt
¼ teaspoon ground black pepper
Leaves from 2 bushy sprigs fresh
  oregano or marjoram, or a few pinches
  dried

Gently break the mushrooms into similarly sized pieces by carefully tugging off large petals or clusters of smaller ones from the stem, or by trimming them lengthwise through the stem.

Combine the oils, vinegar, salt, and pepper in a small saucepan and heat until it begins to simmer. Add the mushrooms, then cover the pan and cook for 2 minutes. Remove from the heat, then stir to incorporate the mushrooms into the liquid. Stir the herb leaves into the mushrooms. Serve warm, or transfer it to a pint container or jar and allow to cool, then store, covered, in the refrigerator for up to 3 days.

MARINATED BEANS WITH SUN-DRIED TOMATOES

Card-carrying member of the Rancho Gordo Bean Club that I am, I always have a tantalizing array of dried beans on hand. And second only to serving them in a little pool of their broth with a drizzle of olive oil, there doesn't come a simpler way to showcase special beans than marinating them. Paired with rehydrated sun-dried tomatoes, a dose of vinegar, and a few dried spices, beans really show their range—going from nutrient-powerhouse comfort food to elegant little antipasti. The marinated beans can function as a dip, scooped into lettuce cups or with chips; as an easy topping for grilled toasts or sturdy crackers; or as a salad either on its own or stretched with diced avocado, ripe tomatoes, and/or a few handfuls of leafy herbs or tender salad greens. And while I like brown beans here, meaning those that are pinto-adjacent, any medium-sized bean that holds its shape well after cooking will do.

Makes about 1½ cups

4 sun-dried tomatoes (not oil-packed)
3 tablespoons olive oil
3 plump cloves garlic, thinly sliced
½ teaspoon crushed red pepper flakes
1½ cups cooked white or brown
    beans, in their broth (see below for
    instructions)

2 teaspoons red wine vinegar
Freshly ground black pepper
Kosher salt
Fresh chives, parsley, cilantro, or
    oregano, for serving

Place the sun-dried tomatoes in a heat-safe bowl and cover with boiling water. Let stand until softened, 10 to 15 minutes or more. Then drain and slice the tomatoes into thin strips.

In a medium skillet, warm the olive oil, garlic, and pepper flakes over low heat. Cook gently, until the garlic is softened and becoming translucent. Add the sun-dried tomatoes and cook for a few minutes more, allowing them to mingle with the garlic and chilies, followed by the beans, including a bit of the bean broth if using home-cooked beans. Raise the heat slightly and leave over the heat until the beans are warmed through, 5 to 10 minutes (avoid bringing the mixture to a simmer, which might cause some of the beans to break). Stir in the vinegar and a few grinds of pepper, as well as salt to taste.

Remove from the heat and transfer the entire contents of the skillet to a jar or other heat-safe container to cool. Allow to marinate for at least a few hours before serving, or once cooled, seal with a lid and store in the refrigerator for up to a week—over time the flavors will become more pronounced. Bring them back to room temperature before serving. Garnish with a sprinkle of fresh chopped herbs.

(cont.)

Tangy-Juicy | Pickles + Marinades

To Cook Beans in an Electric Pressure Cooker: Soak 1 cup dried beans in plenty of water overnight. Drain and transfer to the bowl of an electric pressure cooker. Cover with water by about 2 inches, then add 1 teaspoon salt, and any aromatics you please (2 to 3 tablespoons olive oil, bay leaves, a square of kombu, half of an onion, 2 to 3 smashed garlic cloves, a dried whole chili, etc.). Seal the lid and close the pressure valve, then cook the beans on high pressure for 18 minutes. Allow the pressure to release naturally, or for at least 15 minutes, then check doneness. Every batch of beans has a different cooking time, and while there is nothing good at all about undercooked beans, it can be easy to overcook them in the pressure cooker; if they're not tender, cook again on high pressure for 5 to 10 minutes, again allowing the pressure to release naturally or for at least 15 minutes.

To Cook Beans on the Stovetop: Soak 1 cup of dried beans in plenty of water overnight. Drain and transfer to a pot or medium saucepan. Cover with water by about 2 inches, then add 1 teaspoon salt, and any aromatics you please (2 to 3 tablespoons olive oil, bay leaves, a square of kombu, half of an onion, 2 to 3 smashed garlic cloves, a dried whole chili, etc.). Bring to a boil, then reduce the heat to a gentle simmer, partially cover the pan, and cook them until tender. Start checking for doneness after 30 minutes, though they may cook for up to 90 minutes, and continue sampling until tender. You may need to add additional water to keep the beans submerged.

MARINATED GOAT CHEESE OR FETA

Give your soft, tangy, fresh goat cheese or creamy feta a minor makeover by simply marinating it in flavorful oil and aromatics. Of course this makes a great addition to a cheese platter, but I tend to prefer serving marinated cheeses alongside a few pickled vegetables or crudités, some bread, a hard-boiled egg, and a scoop of a spoon salad, bringing decadence to a snacky meal. A creamy-textured cheese makes a big difference—many goat cheeses are creamy and will hold their shape (aside from the spreadable ones, which are too soft, and the aged ones, which are too hard), but for feta, I find Bulgarian feta to be the best. It's usually packaged in-house at the grocery store, in a pint container with its brine. Try to find a feta that comes packed in brine and, if Bulgarian isn't available, just look for one made in Greece. There's a lot of flexibility with the simple method, which is why I've written the recipe out to be more of a blueprint than a rule book.

Makes 2 to 3 cups

8 ounces soft goat cheese or creamy feta
Oil to submerge: olive oil, nut oil, or a
    combination
Whole dried aromatics: peppercorns,
    fennel seeds, cumin seeds, coriander
    seeds, bay leaves, cardamom pods,
    allspice berries, mustard seeds

1–2 whole dried chilies or a few pinches
    chili flakes
A few sprigs fragrant fresh herbs:
    oregano, thyme, marjoram, dill
Strips of citrus zest, made using a
    vegetable peeler: orange or lemon

Cut, break, or roll the cheese into bite-sized pieces or balls.

In the jar or container you plan to store the cheese in, pour a thin layer of oil over the bottom. Add the dried aromatics and dried chili. Arrange a layer of the cheese pieces, and drizzle with oil. Continue layering in the cheese and drizzling with oil until you've worked through all the cheese. Last, tuck in the herbs and citrus strips. Seal the container.

Allow to marinate for at least an hour before serving, but for best results allow at least a day for flavors to develop. Bring to room temperature before serving.

Suggested Pairings

- Feta + 1 teaspoon peppercorns + 1 teaspoon coriander seeds + 2 whole dried chilies + strips of lemon zest + oregano sprigs
- Goat cheese or feta + 2 teaspoons fennel seeds + pinch chili flakes + strips of orange zest
- Feta + 1 teaspoon cumin seeds + 1 teaspoon fennel seeds + strips of lemon zest
- Goat cheese + ½ teaspoon black peppercorns + ½ teaspoon allspice berries + star anise + bay leaf
- Goat cheese or feta + big pinch dried chili + 2 to 3 thyme sprigs + strips of lemon zest

WARM, REVIVED OLIVES

I feel lucky to live in New York City for all sorts of reasons, and among them is the fact that olive bars are common at grocery stores. They make it easy to scope out the quality of the olives, but also present a range of different varieties and the option to mix and match as you please—rather than having to buy them by the jar. If you've got access to an olive bar (and I've been happy to see them become more common in supermarkets across the country), try to buy them there for this recipe. Avoid the ones sold in oil-based marinades already—brine-packed are best. Rinsing them of the brine freshens their flavor, and warming them in fresh olive oil softens their flesh just enough to make them extra juicy. It's a small, easy step that will turn them into an addictive addition to your snack spread.

Makes 1 cup

1 cup firm-fleshed, shiny olives stored in brine, any variety	1 teaspoon fennel seeds
	½ teaspoon dried chili flakes
2 tablespoons good olive oil	1 strip orange zest
3 short rosemary sprigs	2 tablespoons fresh orange juice

Place the olives in a colander or sieve and rinse under cold running water for about 15 seconds, then blot dry with a clean kitchen towel or paper towel.

Just before you're ready to serve, warm the olive oil, rosemary, fennel seeds, and chili flakes in a small saucepan or skillet over low heat, just until fragrant. Stir in the olives and heat for another 5 minutes, until the olives are slightly softened and heated through. Add the orange zest and heat for another minute, then transfer the entire contents to a shallow bowl for serving. Stir in the orange juice and serve. These are best served warm, but can be stored in an airtight container in the refrigerator for up to 3 days.

Mom + the Sanctity of a Recipe

My mom learned to cook from cookbooks, food magazines, and recipes passed around among her friends. She liked to annotate the recipes she tried, largely from Junior League cookbooks, with notes like *GREAT!* and *O.K.*, and in one of our kitchen cupboards, she kept a stack of manilla file folders that were always held together by threads at the seams, due to being so crammed full of her recipe clippings and xeroxes. Those folders may have been organized by some private method, but whenever she needed something in there, it required retrieving all the folders and sorting through most of their contents until she flipped to the one she was looking for. She was also old enough that she had personalized recipe cards with FROM THE KITCHEN OF PAM VOLGER printed across the tops, though I didn't ever know her to use them for recipes as often as scraps of paper or the backs of envelopes. I'm making it sound like she was a chaotic cook, but she wasn't—she just really liked recipes, and dutifully held on to them.

When I started showing an interest in cooking and food, Mom brought me into her fold. On summer evenings, we'd station ourselves in lawn chairs placed squarely in the sunny stretch of the backyard, with a stack of magazines between us. We'd flip through them cover to cover, sometimes remarking on the recipes that caught our eye, but mostly we didn't talk, just sat there listening to the rustling sounds of leaves or grass in the wind, and pages turning or being ripped out as new recipes were added to her folders. As the light shifted, we'd drag the chairs a few feet across the lawn to stay in the path of the sun, and once it went down, it was time to go back inside.

We never had a copy of *Mastering the Art of French Cooking* or a subscription to *Gourmet* or *Saveur*—what Mom read was *Cooking Light, Woman's Day, Redbook,* and sometimes *Bon Appétit.* At some point in the late '90s, we started to pay attention to the Food Network, and her friend Wendy Meilke introduced us to Ina Garten, whose flag cake and effortless entertaining style seized both our imaginations. A shift took place during this period, as we took a keener interest in salt-and-pepper-style preparations, and fresh citrus juice, and we pretended that we'd never been the types to buy the big jars of pre-minced garlic at Costco. But regardless of how her cooking evolved, it was always tethered to a recipe.

So it made sense that she was such an ardent collector: She followed them to the letter. She didn't like to improvise in the kitchen—she wouldn't even eyeball a measurement. She seemed to believe that some things were just beyond her skill set, or even cursed (such as yeast—she skipped right past any recipe that called for yeast). But when a recipe was good and it *did* work, it became canon. There were lots of these dishes—Shirley Allen casserole, Mexican Lasagna, the Quiche Lorraine from *Bound to Please* (by the Junior League of Boise), the Spinach Salad with Warm Bacon Vinaigrette from *Beyond Parsley* (by the Junior League of Denver). They formed the backbone of both her entertaining and weeknight cooking alike.

A lot of this probably sounds familiar, since plenty of home cooks—particularly the ones tasked with feeding families day in and day out, as my mom did—aren't inclined to waste limited time and ingredients conducting experiments in their kitchens. When something worked, it worked, and Mom was always adding to her arsenal, building an increasingly robust collection of dishes to suit her needs. When she'd try a new recipe, following it closely as she always did, and it didn't work out as she'd expected it to, she'd always question herself first. Was it an error she'd made? Perhaps. But she wouldn't try making it again.

As a young cook, I once believed that "real" cooks used recipes only as inspiration, and that a "real" cook had to add something new to a recipe in order to make it interesting. But now, when I think of Mom and her collection of recipes, I see extra clearly that a recipe isn't just an idea or a jumping-off point or a loose guide, but rather a pact. Her favorite recipes established trust and gave her confidence.

Mom passed away in 2005, and it wasn't until after she died that I started writing recipes professionally. I often wish I could return her gift to me by showing her *my* food fold, my version of the lawn chairs in the sun in the backyard, which would be hanging out in the kitchen conducting experiments. I wish that I could brainstorm ideas with her, involve her in the recipe testing, and share in the thrill of being able to do this work at all. And I'd want to know what marks (*O.K., EXCELLENT, VERY GOOD*) she'd jot down in this book. In absence of that, I have to hope she'd be proud and perhaps pleased that I try to honor the part of her legacy that was her love of recipes—the pleasure she took in collecting them, the value she bestowed, and how she always approached them in such a spirit of curiosity and faith.

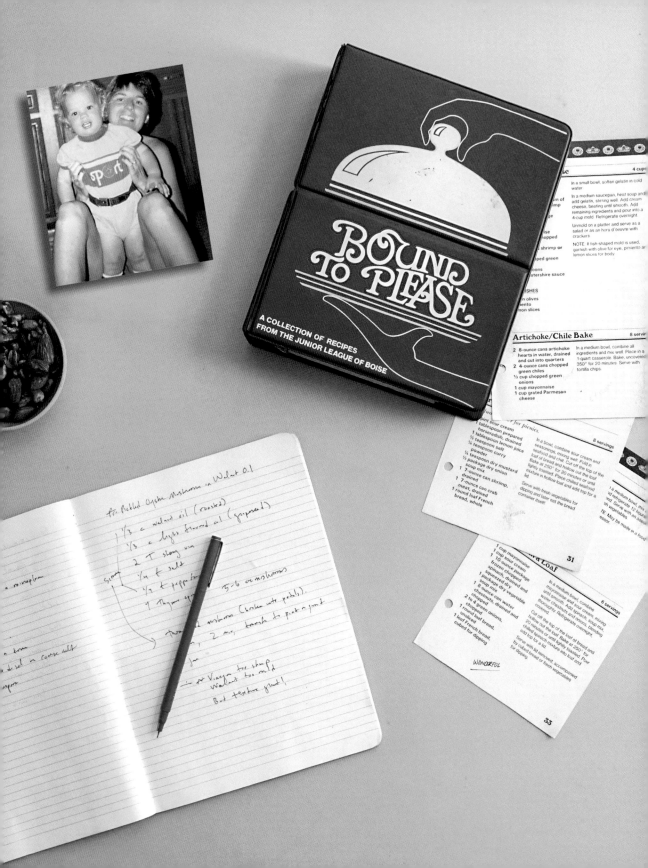

SCOOPED + SMEARED | DIPS + SPREADS

Dip! The word practically requires an exclamation point. Dip is fun! Dip is a party! Dip is a sigh of relief, because with dip at the table, you can let your pretenses down a little. That's always been my experience, anyway. In fact, "dip" was largely synonymous with "appetizer" when I was growing up—no gathering was complete without something to drag a potato chip through, which I still believe to be solid party advice.

But dip can also be dinner. I learned this in a most visceral way during the height of the COVID-19 pandemic, when the slog of all the cooking at home got to a point where assembling dinner became an exercise in dirtying as few dishes as possible. In this way, dinner was the fridge emptied out, all the food storage containers doubling as servingware, and chips and pitas and other edible vessels standing in as forks. Dip nudged toward the center of the plate to become dinner's central hub—the rest of the meal building from there.

These are my greatest-hits dips, starting with the Mixed Mushroom Pâté that's been a New Year's Eve staple for almost a decade. Nut and seed butter shines through the chapter, from a spicy spread fragrant with the heat of dried chili to a gingery tahini dip, as does cheese—from a tangy cottage cheese dip influenced by the flavors of gribiche, to a whipped blend of toasted walnuts and feta cheese that might bring to mind the idea of "savory frosting." I also share a terrific nondairy alternative to creamy, fresh but still tangy cheese in Cultured Cashew Ricotta, which doubles as a flavor block recipe elsewhere in the book. Make a few of these dips for stowing away in the fridge, and know that you'll always be just a chip or cracker away from having dinner ready.

Note: Pureed or whipped bean-, nut-, and some cheese-based dips will often firm up in the refrigerator. To revive the texture, return them to the food processor or blender and rewhip them.

Beyond Snacks for Dinner

One of my favorite methods for serving dips is to treat them as a smear beneath a salad. Simply dollop a spoonful or two over a shallow bowl or salad plate, use the back of the spoon to evenly smear it around, and pile your salad on top. This works well for grain or lentil salads, as well as for those made of tender leafy greens—by adding some richness, body, and surprise.

Scooped + Smeared | Dips + Spreads

MIXED MUSHROOM PÂTÉ

This vegetarian pâté delivers multipronged richness, featuring a cashew base, caramelized onions, miso, and deep mushroom flavor. I've been making it for years, and used to be adamant that a little bit of heavy cream (and some butter) was necessary here. But I've since evolved to think this vegan version—where a small amount of tahini provides the creamy mouthfeel—is superior. If you don't want to splurge on porcini mushrooms, I often make this using other dried mushrooms, such as hen of the woods, wood ear, and black trumpet mushrooms, and a "forest" medley also works terrifically. Slather the leftovers on toasts or crackers, serve with crudités, or use it as sandwich filling.

Makes about 2 cups

1 cup raw cashews	½ teaspoon kosher salt
½ ounce (about ½ cup) dried porcini mushrooms, or other dried mushrooms (see above)	8 ounces cremini or button mushrooms (about 2½ cups), coarsely chopped
3 tablespoons olive oil	2 tablespoons brandy or whiskey
1 medium onion, diced	1 tablespoon light-colored miso
2 cloves garlic, peeled and smashed	2 teaspoons tahini
	Freshly ground black pepper

In separate bowls or glasses, cover the cashews and mushrooms with hot tap water for 20 to 30 minutes. The mushrooms should be softened all the way through. Drain and rinse the cashews. Pick out the mushrooms and squeeze, reserving the excess liquid with any left in the soaking vessel, then coarsely chop the mushrooms.

Heat half the oil in a skillet over medium heat. Add the onion, smashed garlic cloves, and a big pinch of salt and cook, stirring periodically, until caramelized, about 15 to 20 minutes, lowering the heat if they start to brown too quickly. Transfer to the bowl of a food processor or high-speed blender.

Return the skillet to the heat and add remaining oil. When warmed, add the fresh mushrooms. Cook for about 5 minutes, until the liquid begins to pool in the pan, then add the chopped porcini mushrooms and cook for another 5 to 7 minutes, until the pan has dried out. Pour in the alcohol and cook until the pan is dry. Add to the onions.

Add the remaining ingredients to the mushrooms and onions and process until very smooth, which will take a few minutes, stopping to scrape down the sides periodically. Taste and adjust seasonings. It will thicken as it sits; if the pâté is too thick to move, add the reserved mushroom soaking liquid by the tablespoon with the motor running. Scoop into jars or a container and, once cooled, cover tightly and refrigerate for several hours before serving. It will keep in the fridge for up to 5 days.

TOASTED WALNUT + FETA DIP

This creamy, savory dip brings big flavor in small bites, and is also somehow the perfect excuse to eat a whole block of cheese in one sitting. We included it in our wedding snack box (page 151) because it's so distinctive, the toasted nuts lending an earthy counterpoint to the creamy, tangy, and rich cheese. The brine-packed feta is superior here, not only because the brine can be necessary as an ingredient, but because it's more moist than dry-packed feta and will result in a creamier dip. If you can only find dry-packed feta, add a tablespoon of milk along with the cheese, and then use 2 to 3 tablespoons more milk to lighten the consistency as needed. And when toasting the nuts, push them to the limit. You don't want them burnt, but you do want them toasted all the way through for maximum flavor.

Makes about 2 cups

1 cup coarsely chopped walnuts

10.5 ounces feta packed in brine, brine reserved

Zest from 1/2 lemon

Freshly ground black pepper

1½ teaspoons olive oil, plus extra for drizzling

1 teaspoon oregano

Pinch red pepper flakes

Pinch coarse or flaky salt

Preheat the oven to 350°F, and spread the walnuts out on an oven-safe skillet or small baking sheet. Toast for 15 to 20 minutes, until deeply browned and quite fragrant. You're looking for a well-toasted nut here, as they're a major flavor vehicle for the dip. Cool and set aside ¼ cup of the nuts to use for topping.

Place the remaining ¾ cup nuts in the bowl of a food processor fitted with a blade and pulse several times until finely chopped. Add the feta (reserving its brine), breaking it up into smaller pieces, as well as the lemon zest and several grinds of black pepper, and then process until smooth. The mixture will eventually coalesce into a ball, and then smooth out into a thick paste, and you'll need to scrape the sides and bottom of the bowl a few times as you go. With the motor running, add 2 tablespoons of the reserved feta brine, or milk, if your feta is not brine-packed. Add another tablespoon in the same manner, if you prefer a lighter dip.

To make the topping, stir together the reserved walnuts with the 1½ teaspoons olive oil, the oregano, the pepper flakes, and the flaky salt.

To serve, scrape the dip into a serving bowl. Create a little divot in the center and fill with the walnut mixture. Drizzle with olive oil and serve.

Stored in an airtight container, the dip will keep for about 5 days in the refrigerator. Store the walnut topping separately.

TOASTED CHILI-NUT BUTTER SPREAD

This dip is an adaptation of the spicy peanut dip from Deborah Madison's *Vegetarian Cooking for Everyone* that I've been making for years. It's an unexpectedly full-flavored spread that, as she says, "makes even the most mundane crudités irresistible." I also like it as the basis of a peanut butter sandwich (my Peanut Butter & Greens Sandwich in *Start Simple* is a great place for it) or smeared on a cracker. The recipe has gone through some evolutions, and now includes a base of toasted and reconstituted dried red chilies, which gives the dip a brick-like color and deep, dry warmth. Experiment with other dried chilies if you can't find anchos—just try to choose a mild one, and if you aren't sure about its heat or flavor, break off a little piece of the flesh and test its heat level. Large ones like anchos and pasillas are often quite mild. I always seed them in blended dips because even with a mild chili, cracking open the seeds during blending can easily unload too much heat.

Makes about 1 cup

2 dried ancho chilies (see headnote)	1 tablespoon maple syrup
¾ teaspoon kosher salt	2 scallions, green and white parts,
1 cup unsweetened peanut, almond, or	sliced thinly
cashew butter	Juice and zest of 1 lime

Cut or snip the chilies open to remove the seeds and discard the stems. Heat a dry skillet over medium-high heat, and once it's hot, add them to the pan, using a spatula to press them flat onto the surface. Cook until they soften slightly and start to look a bit shimmery, which will take only around a minute. Transfer to a heat-safe bowl and cover with hot water. Let stand until softened and pliable, about 15 minutes. Fish the chilies from the water (reserve the water), and cut them into smaller pieces.

In a food processor, blitz the chilies with the salt to further mince them, then add the nut butter and maple syrup. Process until well combined—the mixture should be thick and even crumbly at this point. With the motor running, add the reserved chili-soaking water in a steady stream until the mixture lightens in color and takes on a whipped consistency. You'll need between ⅓ and ⅔ cup. Taste, adding additional salt as needed.

To serve, smear the dip on a plate or shallow bowl, then garnish with the scallions, lime zest, and a spritz of lime juice. Stored in an airtight container in the refrigerator, it'll keep for up to 5 days.

Lemony Fried Chickpeas (p. 49)

Whipped Fresh Ricotta (p. 88)

FRESH RICOTTA

If you've never made ricotta before, it'll be a thrill to discover that something so delicious can be so straightforward—you're just heating milk until it almost comes to a boil, adding acid to separate it into curds and whey, and then straining the mixture. Traditionally, cheesemongers would make it from whey (the byproduct from making other cheeses) rather than milk or cream, but that assumes that you've got a bunch of whey lying around. This homemade version is so rich and special that it can serve as its own centerpiece in a snacks-for-dinner spread. Just flesh it out with some toasts, plenty of crudités, a few jammy boiled eggs, and some crunchy nuts or seeds. This kind of recipe is flexible—you may want to double the recipe for a higher yield, but I usually make it when I've got too much milk on hand and it's nearing its expiration date. It works best with 4 cups of milk minimum. And if there's cream or half-and-half lingering around, throw that in there for a richer ricotta, up to 25 percent of the quantity of milk you're using. There are hundreds of simple ways to gussy it up as an easy appetizer, and I've included some of my favorites below. Last thing: To make an excellent dip using store-bought ricotta, simply blend it in your food processor as instructed below. It works best with good-quality ricotta that's creamy to begin with.

Makes about 2 cups

2 quarts whole milk	3 to 4 tablespoons fresh lemon juice, or
1 teaspoon kosher salt	more if needed

Combine the milk and salt in a medium saucepan and place over medium heat. You need to bring it to about 190°F, which is the point when it's steaming abundantly but, importantly, has not yet come to a boil. It's not imperative to use a thermometer, though it does make things easier to gauge as the mixture heats up. Stir often, both to prevent scorching on the bottom as well as to keep a skin from forming on the top, which will cause the whole thing to foam over.

Remove from the heat, add 3 tablespoons lemon juice, and let stand for about 5 minutes for curds to firm up. If the mixture doesn't begin to curdle within 30 seconds or a minute, add another tablespoon of lemon juice. (If it still doesn't curdle, continue adding more lemon juice by the tablespoon.) While waiting, set a sieve or colander over a large bowl and line it with cheesecloth.

Pour the mixture through the cheesecloth, making sure the base of the sieve or colander completely clears the whey and isn't suspended in any liquid. Let stand for 20 to 30 minutes. Check periodically as the whey accumulates, pouring off as needed if it starts to reach the base of the sieve or colander.

(cont.)

The whey can be used as soup stock, as liquid in making bread, in smoothies, and even for cooking beans. Store the ricotta in an airtight container, where it should keep for 2 to 3 days.

Whipped Ricotta

To give ricotta (either homemade or store-bought) a light, airy consistency that's perfect for dolloping and swooping, blitz it in a food processor until smooth. If it's so well-strained that it simply becomes crumbles or a thick paste, add whey or milk by the tablespoon, until it becomes creamy.

Serving Suggestions for Ricotta

Smear a generous amount of ricotta over a serving plate or in a shallow bowl, and use a spoon to create a well in the center. Then add any of the following:

- Umami Roasted Tomatoes (page 63) or Crispy Broiled Maitake Mushrooms (page 50)
- Oyster Mushrooms in Walnut Oil (page 68), including a drizzle of the marinade
- Toasted Nuts, Honey or Maple Syrup, and Flaky Salt
- Ripe berries or chopped stone fruit, (plums, peaches, nectarines), a light drizzle of balsamic vinegar, and a light garnish torm basil or tarragon
- Onion Jam (page 90) or Chili-Ginger Jam (page 91)—since these are thicker jams, they're easiest to assemble directly on toast or crackers

CULTURED CASHEW RICOTTA

Adding probiotics to thick, blended cashew cream and leaving it to ferment for a day at room temperature cultures it, helping it to develop some tartness and funk. I love to cook with this cheese and find it to be a great vegan substitute for ricotta, goat cheese, and cream cheese. It appears in Vegan Spinach + Cheese Pierogi (page 145), as a filling for Dates Four Ways (page 216), and when combined with Umami Roasted Tomatoes (page 63), it makes an excellent dip—just smear some ricotta on a plate and spoon the tomatoes over it. When fermenting vegan cheese, it's recommended that you sanitize your equipment and tools by rinsing them with boiling water; I'll admit I haven't done that every time I've made this recipe, but it's a good idea. Metal can interact with the probiotics, which is why you'll fold the probiotics into the mixture rather than blend them; to that end, make sure to store the cheese in a glass or ceramic container rather than a metal one.

Makes about 2 cups

2 cups raw cashews	½ to ¾ cup water
½ teaspoon kosher salt	5 probiotic capsules (acidophilus)

Cover the cashews with room-temperature water and soak for 2 to 6 hours. Drain and rinse, then add to the bowl of a food processor or the pitcher attached to a high-speed blender along with the salt. With the motor running, add ½ cup water in a steady stream. Continue processing until very smooth. You can add up to ¼ cup more water to lighten the consistency. If using a food processor, allow plenty of time to thoroughly process the nuts (a blender will work much more quickly). Stop periodically to scrape the sides. Transfer the mixture to a non-metal bowl.

Shake the contents of the capsules into the cashew mixture (discarding the capsules themselves) and fold to combine. Then scrape the mixture into a 3- to 4-cup glass or ceramic container. Tidy up the sides of the dish and cover with a clean towel, then leave to ferment at room temperature for 18 to 24 hours in a dry, cool space. Stir the cheese (a pale-brown crust will form on the surface, which is normal and safe to eat) and taste. It should have developed some pleasant tanginess. If not tangy enough, leave to ferment for another 12 hours. The temperature of your kitchen is a major factor in how long the fermentation should be—the warmer it is, the faster the ferment. But knowing that it'll develop more flavor in the fridge, and firm up a bit as well, I usually err on the side of less tangy at this stage.

Transfer to an airtight container and store in the refrigerator for up to 2 weeks.

Scooped + Smeared | Dips + Spreads

ONION JAM

This onion jam is sticky and sweet, and because of the playful sparring of savory and sweet happening in the jam itself, it's an excellent one to use in savory treatments. In the Feta + Jam Tart (page 117), the tangles of onion melt and mingle with the cheese, providing a perfect contrast to its salty tartness. And to that end, it's a great accompaniment to a cheese board or as a condiment for a sandwich, particularly a grilled cheese with Gruyere or fontina cheese. While the end product is jam, the process is essentially about caramelizing onions, and it employs a trick that I learned on Instagram from the food writer Ozoz Sokoh, where the pan is covered at first to let the onions steam and begin to cook in their own juices—this dramatically speeds up the process, and it's one to remember the next time you need to cook down a bunch of onions.

Makes about 1½ cups

2 tablespoons butter or olive oil

2 large white or yellow onions, sliced
  into strips about ⅛ inch thick

½ teaspoon kosher salt

¼ cup balsamic vinegar

3 tablespoons brown sugar

1 teaspoon honey

½ teaspoon dried thyme

Freshly ground black pepper

Melt the butter or warm the oil over medium heat in a wide skillet, then stir in the onions and salt. Cover the pan and allow the onions to soften and steam for 10 minutes, then uncover, reduce the heat slightly, and continue cooking until soft and golden, another 20 minutes or more. Stir in the vinegar, brown sugar, honey, thyme, and several grinds of black pepper and simmer, stirring often, until the onions are caramelized and the mixture is thick and sticky, about 20 minutes more. Cool and transfer to an airtight container. Stored in the refrigerator, the jam will keep for up to 2 weeks.

CHILI-GINGER JAM

With the heat of the chilies as well as the ginger, this fragrant, complex jam feels like a burst of sunshine during cold months. I use it to spike the tomato sauce for the Chewy-Crispy Tofu Sticks with Chili-Ginger Jam Dipping Sauce (page 128), but it also works terrifically in all types of marinades and is a great way to change up your peanut butter and jelly sandwich game. It's even excellent spooned into oatmeal. I simplified the process by using the food processor to chop up the vegetables, but for a really attractive jam, and the opportunity to practice your knife skills, finely dice the vegetables by hand.

Makes about 1 cup

1 bell pepper	4 big cloves garlic, coarsely chopped
3 medium-heat red chilies, or jalapeños or serranos	½ teaspoon kosher salt
	½ cup sugar
1 ounce ginger, peeled and coarsely chopped	1 tablespoon apple cider vinegar

Combine the peppers, ginger, garlic, and salt in a food processor and pulse until everything is finely chopped, stopping to scrape the sides and bottom edge of the bowl often and taking care as you pulse to not puree the mixture. (Alternatively, finely dice all the vegetables by hand.) Scrape into a medium saucepan and add the sugar. Bring to a boil and then reduce the heat slightly, to keep the mixture bubbling. Cook for 10 to 15 minutes, until the bubbles go from foamy to clear and big, which means that the water is cooking off. Stir in the vinegar, then remove from the heat and allow to cool slightly. I find it easiest to transfer to a jar while the jam is still warm. Once it cools fully, store in the refrigerator.

Gluten-free Nut
+ Seed Crackers
(p. 194)

Oyster Mushrooms
in Walnut Oil
(p. 68)

Gingery Spinach–Tahini Dip (p. 93)

Honeyed Pickled Shallots (p. 62)

GINGERY SPINACH-TAHINI DIP

I first started making this spicy green dip as a bowl component. Inspired by stylish lunch spots in New York, I'd rub a spoonful across the side of my dish in an artful smear and build the rest of my meal on top of it, using grains and tender greens and various pickled things, where it'd intermingle with the other components as I ate. It's a thick spread, one to set out with a little appetizer knife, and it makes a distinctive option for crackers and crudités. The ginger is sharp, its fresh heat very much on display, and while you'd think that the food processor would do the job of mincing it thoroughly, it's actually important to finely grate the ginger beforehand. Otherwise its fibrous threads—and sometimes larger chunks, which are unpleasant to eat—will find their way into the finished dip.

Makes about 2 cups

10 ounces frozen or fresh spinach	Heaping 1 tablespoon finely grated fresh ginger
½ cup well-stirred tahini	1½ teaspoons maple syrup
	¾ teaspoon kosher salt

If using frozen spinach: Bring a saucepan full of water to boil, then add the spinach (straight out of the freezer; no need to thaw). Cover the pan, and once the water comes back to a boil, the spinach should be thawed. Pour through a sieve. Rinse under cold running water, then squeeze dry.

If using fresh spinach: Fill a pot with an inch of water then fit with a steamer insert. Bring the water to a simmer, then add the spinach and cover the pot. Cook for 2 to 4 minutes, until the spinach has collapsed and is bright green. Transfer it to a sieve or colander and rinse under cold running water, then squeeze dry.

Place the drained spinach in the bowl of a high-speed blender or food processor along with the tahini, ginger, maple syrup, and salt. Process thoroughly, scraping down the sides and bottom of the bowl often. Add 1 tablespoon water at a time as needed to achieve a lighter consistency. Stored in an airtight container, the dip will keep for up to 3 days in the refrigerator.

CHARRED ALLIUM + LABNEH DIP

Using labneh, the thick Middle Eastern yogurt, in this spin on French onion dip makes it feel just as rich, but with more tang and a different style of creamy texture. Greek-style yogurt isn't quite thick enough, but if that's all you can find, I recommend straining it even further for best results (just scoop 1 cup of yogurt into a cheesecloth-lined sieve or colander, and set in the refrigerator overnight, then scoop the thickened yogurt into an airtight container). Broiling the scallions and onion introduces both charred and caramelized notes. The same thing can be achieved on a grill if you have one, and once they're coarsely chopped up, they provide succulent texture in the dip.

Makes about 1½ cups

1 bunch scallions	2 teaspoons fresh lemon juice
½ large or 1 small white or yellow onion	2 teaspoons white wine vinegar
High-smoke-point oil, such as grapeseed or avocado oil	¾ cup labneh
	Freshly ground black pepper
Kosher salt	Olive oil, for drizzling
1 small clove garlic	

Preheat the boiler on its high-heat setting.

Trim the root ends off the scallions, as well as about ¼ inch from the tips. Arrange on one side of a baking sheet. Cut the onion into wedges through the stem about ½ inch thick, and arrange on the other end of the baking sheet. Drizzle with a bit of the high-smoke-point oil and sprinkle with a few pinches of salt.

Place the onions and scallions on the rack closest to the heat source. Checking every 3 minutes, cook until the green parts of the scallions are blistered and charred, and the onions are charred in parts and appear juicy and translucent, flipping them once. It should take 9 to 12 minutes. If the scallions cook more quickly than the onions, remove them, then return the pan to the broiler to continue cooking the onions. Allow to cool until safe to handle.

Meanwhile, in a mortar and pestle, pound the garlic clove with a pinch of salt until it becomes a juicy paste—or mince and mash the garlic and salt on a cutting board, using the flat side of the knife to spread it in a thin layer across the board until you get a paste.

Coarsely chop all the alliums, discarding any root bits if they're still connected to the onion, and transfer to a mixing bowl. Add the garlic paste, lemon juice, and white wine vinegar, stirring to combine. Let stand for about 10 minutes, then stir in the labneh, ¼ teaspoon salt, and a few grinds of pepper. Taste, adding more salt as needed. Serve cold or room temperature, drizzled with olive oil. Stored in an airtight container in the refrigerator, it'll keep for up to 3 days.

Charred Allium + Labne Dip (p. 94)

Crispy Parmesan–
Pecan Strips
(p. 188)

Baked Brussels Sprouts Chips
(p. 45)

Smoky Confit'd Beans with Olives (p. 101)

Pure Green Soup (p. 168)

Creamy Sweet
Potato Chipotle Dip
(p. 97)

CREAMY SWEET POTATO CHIPOTLE DIP

This is a beguiling dip. Just when you think it might be too sweet, it becomes spicy, and then takes on smoky and bright notes as well. It's a *journey,* and all thanks to an incredibly brief list of ingredients. You'll need to roast the sweet potatoes, but if you have leftover roasted sweet potatoes on hand it'll come together in minutes. It works just as well with a plain-flavored vegan cream cheese (I like Miyoko's brand best) or the Cultured Cashew Ricotta (page 89). And while it plays the fun 'n' funky role in a dip-for-dinner spread, I also enjoy dolloping it over grain bowls or using it as a sandwich spread. The leftover chipotle chilies in adobo can be frozen and used for future dishes.

Makes about 1½ cups

2 medium sweet potatoes (6 to 8 ounces each)	6 tablespoons cream cheese or vegan cream cheese
2 canned chipotles in adobo sauce	Juice of 1 lime
½ teaspoon kosher salt	Lime zest, for garnish (optional)

Roast the sweet potatoes: Preheat the oven to 400°F. Rub the skins with a bit of olive oil and sprinkle with salt, then place in a small baking dish or oven-safe skillet. Roast for 45 to 75 minutes, until tender all the way through and the flesh has shriveled a bit inside the skins. Cool until safe to handle.

Pull off the peels, reserving them for another use, and put the flesh in the bowl of a food processor along with the chipotles, up to 2 tablespoons of the adobo sauce, salt, and cream cheese. Process thoroughly, until creamy and smooth. Add half the lime juice and taste, then add more salt and lime juice as needed. The dip will thicken slightly as it cools. Garnish with lime zest to serve, if desired. Stored in an airtight container in the refrigerator, the dip will keep for up to 5 days.

EGGPLANT + CHICKPEA WHIP

This is a more savory, but just as light and very smooth mash-up of my favorite styles of hummus (a tahini-rich one) and moutabbal (or, for years, what I'd thought was baba ganoush—the eggplant and tahini dip that's salty, smooth, and smoky; baba ganoush doesn't traditionally include the tahini). It utilizes a genius trick from my friend and fellow cookbook author Hetty McKinnon, where aquafaba (the liquid from canned chickpeas, or the cooking liquid in home-cooked beans) is blitzed in to lend its volumizing powers. I'd always used warm water to lighten up my hummus, but the aquafaba is one of those *Why didn't I ever think of that?* methods. The dip is rich and flavorful, with a seductive, smoky back note thanks to the broiled eggplant and small amount of miso, but is light enough in texture that you can drag the most delicate crudité through it. Small, Italian-style eggplants work great because they're exactly the right size for this quantity of dip. Large globe eggplants often weigh about three times as much as the smaller one I list below—if you only have one of those, use about ⅓ to ½ of the broiled flesh, and for the best accuracy, weigh the eggplant.

Makes about 3 cups

1 Italian or small globe eggplant (about 8 ounces)	¼ cup well-stirred tahini
	1 tablespoon miso paste
One 15-ounce can chickpeas (or 1¾ cups home-cooked ones, cooking liquid reserved)	1 teaspoon kosher salt
	1 lemon
	Olive oil, for serving

Preheat your broiler on its high-heat setting. Pierce the eggplant a few times all over using a paring knife, then set it on a baking sheet. Cook it directly under the broiler's heat source, flipping every 3 to 4 minutes, until the skin is blackened and crisp, and the vegetable meets almost no resistance when pierced with a paring knife. Allow to cool until safe to handle, then pull off the skin in strips and add the eggplant flesh to a blender pitcher or the bowl of a food processor.

Strain the chickpeas over a tall measuring cup or glass. Reserve the canning liquid.

Add the chickpeas to the eggplant, along with the tahini, miso, salt, and the juice of half the lemon. Blend the mixture and then add up to 5 tablespoons of the chickpea liquid, one tablespoon at a time, until the dip is very smooth and light. Use your judgment—you may not want to add more than 3 tablespoons. Stop to scrape the sides as needed. Taste, adding more salt or lemon as needed.

To serve, smear over a shallow bowl or plate and drizzle with olive oil. In an airtight container in the refrigerator, this dip will keep for up to 3 days.

STOVETOP MAPLE-ALE MUSTARD

My grandmother had a toffee-colored, tempered-glass double boiler that mostly gathered dust while I was growing up. If you're not familiar—since they don't seem very common in households anymore—this contraption looks like two saucepans stacked on top of one another. Water goes into the bottom saucepan, and then you set the other one on top, filled with whatever food you wish to gently cook over the water simmering in the chamber below. I can only remember Mom borrowing the double boiler from my grandma for one use: making honey mustard. She made it for parties where there was a sandwich station with sliced cheese, cold cuts, presliced dinner rolls, and pickles, and it was a thick, sticky mustard that we all loved—always the star sandwich condiment. Since she died I've been unable to track down the recipe she used, let alone find a method that sounded like an approximation. Then I happened upon Alan Bergo's recipe for homemade maple mustard, which he describes as an "old-school, stove top mustard" on his blog *Forager Chef*. It's sweet, which ensures a decent shelf life, and is thickened with eggs, hence the double boiler. His method was just the portal I needed. I realized as I began making mustard this way that Mom's recipe might now strike me as too sweet—so I've created my own version that's got more heat. And in lieu of a double boiler (I don't own one, either), just set a heat-safe bowl over a saucepan of simmering water.

Makes about 1 cup

¼ cup mustard powder, such as Coleman's or Tin Mustard	¼ cup maple syrup
¼ cup apple cider vinegar	2 egg yolks
½ cup brown ale	½ teaspoon kosher salt

In a wide, heat-safe bowl, stir together the mustard powder and the vinegar. Let stand for at least 30 minutes, and up to an hour. Pour the beer into a tall measuring glass to allow some of its carbonation to burn off while the mustard powder hydrates.

Add the beer, maple syrup, egg yolks, and salt to the mustard and whisk until smooth.

Fill a saucepan with about an inch of water and bring to a simmer. Create a double boiler situation by placing the bowl directly over the saucepan, allowing the steam generated by the water to heat the bowl beneath it. Make sure that the bottom of the bowl does not touch the water—if it does, simply pour out some of the water. Cook the mustard over the simmering water, scraping the sides and bottom of the bowl often with a flexible spatula, until thickened to the consistency of hollandaise sauce—about 15 minutes. Remove from the heat and transfer the mustard to a container or jar. Allow to cool, then store in the refrigerator for up to 3 weeks in an airtight container.

SMOKY CONFIT'D BEANS WITH OLIVES

These warm, creamy beans cloaked in smoky, savory olive oil are a quick centerpiece "dip" for a snacky meal, They provide an excellent contrast to cool, tangy, creamy foods like yogurt and mild, soft cheese, as well as crisp vegetables and grilled toasts. I like to use cannellini beans, though chickpeas work well, too, and canned beans are fine. My small, 6-inch skillet fits a can of beans perfectly and doubles as a serving vessel, but any shallow, oven-safe dish (a gratin dish, or other small casserole) will do, or double the recipe for a 10-inch skillet. If the volume of oil gives you pause, feel free to use less, but use enough that the beans are at least a little bit submerged, else they won't take on such a luxuriously creamy texture.

Serves 3 to 4

1¾ cups cooked white beans (or one 15-ounce can, drained and rinsed)

¼ cup kalamata olives, pitted and coarsely minced

3 plump garlic cloves, smashed

1½ teaspoons smoked paprika

1 teaspoon kosher salt

½ cup olive oil

¼ teaspoon dried oregano

Preheat the oven to 400°F.

In a small skillet or other shallow, oven-safe dish, stir together the beans, olives, garlic, paprika, and salt. Pour the oil over the mixture and gently stir to combine. Transfer to the oven and bake for 30 minutes. I don't stir, as I like the chewy crust that forms on the beans at the surface, but you can stir once or twice as it bakes if you prefer a more uniform consistency.

These are best served hot or warm, garnished with the dried oregano. Leftovers can be stored in an airtight container, where they'll continue to marinate for up to 3 days. Bring to room temperature, or warm, before serving.

ELEMENTAL GUACAMOLE

Guacamole is one of those things I've always made without a recipe. It feels like it ought to be intuitive, since it's just about embellishing a few good, ripe avocados. And yet I always get asked for one when I serve it, so here it is. I think there are three tips that make it stand out. The first is to let the onion pickle slightly in the lime juice and some salt, which blunts some of its raw edge. The second is to leave plenty of texture in it, resisting the urge to mash the fruits as you stir—if they're properly ripe, a creamy dip will form just from stirring. Finally, the third is to salt the guacamole properly! So often homemade versions are underseasoned, which just takes away from the pure decadence of such a dip. Taste as you go, and add salt until it becomes completely addictive. I'm not a fan of tomato here, so I leave it out, but I'll confess that I occasionally use torn basil in place of cilantro, and I do love it.

Makes 3 to 4 cups

$^1/_3$ cup finely minced red onion, from about a quarter of a medium bulb
Kosher salt
1 to 2 limes
4 ripe avocados

1 or 2 serrano chilies, seeded and finely diced
$^2/_3$ cup coarsely chopped cilantro leaves and stems (or basil)

Place the minced onion in a medium mixing bowl. Sprinkle with two big pinches of salt and add the juice of one lime. Stir to combine, then let stand for 5 to 10 minutes so the onion ever-so-slightly pickles.

Cut each avocado in half and remove the pit. Score a crosshatch pattern into each avocado half using your knife, then scoop out the flesh into the bowl with the onions using a spoon. Add the serrano.

Stir everything together. If your avocados are properly ripe, a "sauciness" will form as you stir the mixture, and you won't necessarily need to mash it. Taste for lime juice and salt. It's a good idea to taste the guacamole with the chips you plan to serve alongside, so as to make sure to salt the dip properly. Last, stir in the cilantro. Serve immediately.

Spicy Celery Margarita (p. 206)

My Ideal Focaccia (p. 185)

Cottage Cheese
Gribiche (p. 105)

Dill + White Bean Spread (p. 106)

COTTAGE CHEESE GRIBICHE

Growing up, one appetizer that stood out to my brother and me was steamed artichokes. They were a special treat, and always such a curious vegetable, the flavor and texture so appealing, but such a small return on the investment. We loved them, but I wonder if maybe what we responded most to was that artichoke leaves make terrific dip vessels. Using the lemon-pepper cottage cheese dip my mom used to make as inspiration, I've given cottage cheese sauce the gribiche treatment. It pairs terrifically with cold, steamed artichokes, and all manner of crudités and crackers, too.

Makes about 1½ cups

2 eggs	2 tablespoons capers, rinsed and
2 tablespoons Dijon mustard	coarsely chopped
1 tablespoon white wine vinegar	¼ cup cornichons, coarsely chopped
2 tablespoons olive oil	¼ cup minced parsley
1 cup cottage cheese	Kosher salt, as needed
1 Persian cucumber, finely diced	Freshly ground black pepper, to taste

Bring a saucepan of water to boil, then add the eggs. As soon as the water comes back to boil, reduce the heat to a gentle simmer and cook the eggs for 9 minutes. Transfer to a bowl of ice water to halt the cooking, then when they're safe to handle, peel them, slice in half, and separate the yolks from the whites. Coarsely chop the egg whites and set aside.

In a mixing bowl, mash together the yolks, mustard, and vinegar. Then, while whisking, add the oil in a steady stream, encouraging the mixture to emulsify. Then fold in the remaining ingredients, including the egg whites, and add additional salt if needed. Stored in an airtight container in the refrigerator, the dip will keep for 3 days.

How to Steam Artichokes

Fill a mixing bowl with water and add the juice of 2 lemons. With a serrated knife, or a sharp chef's knife, slice off the top quarter of each artichoke, then use kitchen shears to snip the sharp, pointy parts of the remaining outer leaves. Use a vegetable peeler to remove the skin from the stem. Toss the prepped artichokes into the bowl as you work to prevent them from oxidizing. In a large pot or Dutch oven, insert a steaming basket and add an inch of water. Bring to a simmer, then add the artichokes, cover the pot, and cook until you can easily tug off an outer leaf, 25 to 35 minutes. Drain and allow the artichokes to cool, then chill thoroughly.

DILL + WHITE BEAN SPREAD

This pâté-like vegan dip is thick and creamy, and I like it best when made with butter beans (also known as lima beans) for their slightly less starchy texture, but any canned white bean—cannellini, navy, great northern—will do. Given that dill is such an underused herb in American kitchens, it delights me to throw a whole bunch into this dip, but those who aren't as enthusiastic about it may want to swap in parsley. Either herb will give the dip a lovely, pale-green hue as well as its fresh, defining flavor, which complements pretty much any type of vessel. Soaking the sunflower seeds here softens them just enough to blend in seamlessly, and you can use either roasted seeds or raw ones; the former will bring more of a toasty flavor to the finished dip.

Makes 2 heaping cups

¾ cup hulled sunflower seeds
3 tablespoons olive oil, divided, plus additional for drizzling
1 large leek, sliced thinly
¾ teaspoon kosher salt, plus an additional pinch
2 tablespoons white wine, or vermouth (or water)

One 15-ounce can white beans, drained and rinsed
1 small bunch dill, tough stems removed, a few fronds reserved for garnish
Zest and juice of 1 lemon

Put the sunflower seeds in a bowl or tall measuring glass and cover with hot tap water. Allow to soak for 10 to 20 minutes, then drain and rinse.

Meanwhile, warm 2 tablespoons of the olive oil in a medium skillet over medium-low heat, and add the leek and a big pinch of salt. Sauté, stirring often, until soft, 6 to 8 minutes, turning down the heat if it starts to brown. Pour in the wine or vermouth, scraping up anything that may have stuck to the bottom, then stir in the beans and allow to simmer for a few minutes. Remove from the heat and let cool slightly.

Drain and rinse the sunflower seeds, then put them in the bowl of a food processor or blender along with the beans, leeks, and remaining salt. Process until smooth, adding water by the tablespoon if necessary to get the mixture moving. With the motor running, drizzle in the remaining 1 tablespoon olive oil. Add the dill and process until it's blitzed into the mixture and turned it a pale green. Add lemon zest and 1 tablespoon lemon juice, then taste and adjust as needed, with salt and additional lemon.

Smear the pâté over a shallow bowl or plate, and drizzle generously with olive oil and a few dill fronds. Stored in an airtight container, the dip will keep for 3 days.

How to Crudités

The saying "we eat with our eyes" violates my preference for function over aesthetics—also, some of the most delicious food is ugly!—but when it comes to crudités, there's truth to it. I've learned that if you put care into your crudités, making sure not only that they're fresh and delicious but that they *look* fresh and delicious, people will eat them in no time. See below for some of my favorite ways to prepare specific vegetables. But first, a few tips.

1. **Try to choose vegetables at their seasonal peak.** Often you can get away with some grocery-store options—such as with radishes, Persian cucumbers, endive, and gem lettuces—but with other items, there's a marked improvement in sourcing seasonally. Carrots, fennel, cucumbers, sweet peppers, and tomatoes will be more vibrant in season.

2. **Texture is key.** For carrots, radishes, cucumbers, crunchy lettuces, for example, you can enhance the crunchiness by soaking them in ice water for 10 minutes. (This is also a useful way to revive any vegetables that are starting to go a little limp.) Heartier vegetables need to be cooked or lightly pickled to make them palatable—green beans, asparagus, cauliflower, broccoli. Cool them by shocking in an ice bath so that they stay *just cooked* rather than going mushy.

3. **Fun, irregular shapes pique curiosity.** This is where "eating with our eyes" really comes in—variety invites the eye to linger. Big radishes can be sliced into rounds; smaller ones can be served whole or halved—and leave the greens attached if they're fresh and perky, because they bring color and contrast (and are also delicious).

4. **Add accents.** Just a few little scoops of vegetables that have been "treated" (i.e., marinated, pickled, or otherwise heartily seasoned) can break things up a bit: quick pickles, marinated mushrooms, artichoke hearts, or beans. Tender, leafy herbs, like mint, basil, and shiso, can also be tucked in and function as a palate refresher.

5. Function is the most important thing. If we eat with our eyes, then what we see must tell a story. There needs to be logic; it needs to be intuitive. These vegetables need to be (a) pleasant to eat out of hand, (b) vibrantly displayed, and (c) optimized as a dip vessel. Approach each vegetable keeping in the forefront of your mind what its purpose is. Long, skinny carrot sticks, for example, are fine for dipping into a thin tahini dip, but for a thicker dip it's best to create more surface area on the carrot, to allow for scooping.

ASPARAGUS: These must be cooked, of course—snap off woody ends, steam until just tender, 1 to 3 minutes depending on thickness, then shock in an ice bath. Leave whole.

BROCCOLI OR CAULIFLOWER: Try to trim so that florets are attached to long stems. Steam or parboil until just tender, usually 4 to 6 minutes, then shock in an ice-water bath to preserve the color and stop the cooking. Really large florets can be halved or quartered through the stem.

CARROTS: I don't find it to be necessary to peel carrots, especially when they're organic and fresh. Cut thick carrots on the bias into slabs. Slice thin carrots in half lengthwise. If still attached to greens, and they're attractive and perky, leave a half inch or so attached.

CELERY: Trim long stalks into sticks, but vary the length, and for thick pieces, trim in half at an angle lengthwise. Serve tender hearts (the best part!) with leaves still attached.

CUCUMBERS: Cucumbers with tender skin (like Persian and Armenian cucumbers) don't need to be peeled, but hothouse and other conventional varieties should be peeled. Combine a mix of rounds (sliced on the bias), chunked, and quartered or halved thick pieces.

ENDIVE: Slice off the base end of the endive and gently pluck off the outer leaves, repeating until you get to a tight core. Quarter the core.

FENNEL: Trim off the stalks and then slice the bulb in half through the core. Carefully trim out the core, then, with the cut side down, slice into strips.

KOHLRABI: An otherworldly-looking vegetable that you'll probably only find at the farmers' market, kohlrabi has a quenching crunch. The thick, fibrous skin on mature vegetables should be trimmed off, but when the vegetable is younger, it doesn't need to be peeled. Cut into rounds, wedges, or matchsticks, and sprinkle with salt.

LETTUCES: Little gem lettuces are best here. Save large lettuce leaves for salad—serve only small, close-to-the-heart, crisp leaves that are sturdy enough to carry dip. Once the leaves become too small to serve as dip vessels, quarter the hearts.

POD BEANS: Trim or zip off the stem end of each bean, and then briefly blanch in salted water—just a minute or two, to take off the raw edge but retain its crunch. Shock in ice water, blot dry, then serve whole.

POTATOES: Small, waxy potatoes are best because they hold their shape well and are easy to eat out of hand. Boil or steam in salted water until tender, then chill thoroughly. Serve small potatoes whole or halved, and large ones can be sliced into quarters or eighths. Potatoes are especially good tossed lightly with wine vinegar.

RADISHES AND BABY TURNIPS: Serve these with their perky greens still attached, but trim off any yellowed or browned ones, and use a paring knife to gently scrape off any browned bit around the stems. Halve or quarter large radishes through the stem; serve small ones whole. Very large radishes can be sliced into rounds, and extremely pungent Asian radishes, like daikon—which should be sliced into thin rounds—can be tamed slightly by soaking for 20 minutes in salt water. Store in ice water until serving to prevent drying out.

SWEET PEPPERS: Small peppers can be halved through the stem and don't need to be seeded. For large ones, cut through the stem and trim out the seeds and ribs, then cut into thick, angular wedges or strips.

TOMATOES: The best tomatoes for crudités are small, one-bite cherry ones—anything too large to eat whole, out of hand, doesn't work very well. Aim for a variety of colors.

CENTERPIECE-ISH | A LITTLE HEARTIER

It might seem antithetical to a snacks-for-dinner meal that there be a *main* dish, and to think of these "centerpiece-ish" recipes in that Western-traditional sense—as the "protein," to be buttressed by two sides—isn't right. There are so many cuisines where vegetables are simply more prevalent than they are in the West, where meat assumes a minor role in everyday cooking, and while there are lots of reasons for this (meat being an expensive luxury; religious principles; strong connections to agricultural traditions), I also think a big part just comes down to the plate structuring. A meal can consist of several small things just as easily as it can a few big things, and the former approach simply increases the opportunity to incorporate vegetables.

So while these recipes are not "mains," they are a little bit heartier. You'll find thick slabs of Zucchini Slice—an Australian café staple that's something between a frittata and a savory quick bread—and homemade, herb-centric seasoning salts that effortlessly dress up avocado wedges or boiled eggs, two snack items that I always find to be helpful in filling me up. And since no book of mine is complete without at least a nod to the veggie burger, you'll find veggie burger sliders made from sunflower seeds and quinoa, which seem to get even better as they cool. There are also three hearty(-ish), very different savory tarts, featuring vegetables, fruits, and cheese, that hopefully offer a therapeutic cooking moment in the preparation, since the tactile nature of rolling out crusts always feels that way to me.

Additionally, whether in the kitchen or at the table, many of these dishes are more like activities—main "events" over main courses—lending an interactive feature to the snacks-for-dinner table. Both the homemade pierogi stuffed with a "cheesy" spinach filling, and the arancini balls oozing with melted mozzarella or fontina, are fun for involving your guests in the assembly. Each dinner guest gets to make their own hand rolls at the table, stuffed with an array of colorful vegetables as they please, and both the Chewy-Crispy Tofu Sticks with Chili-Ginger Jam Dipping Sauce and the farinata adorned with a few fistfuls of shredded chicory are best served fresh out of the skillet, while they're still warm.

Beyond Snacks for Dinner

Many of these recipes—particularly the make-ahead ones—are excellent picnic food, and great for packed lunches. And since these dishes are heartier than some of the others, they all function well as vegetarian options in potlucks and other large, celebratory meals.

FETA + JAM TART

About fifteen years ago, I took a cooking class in Paris with renowned teacher Paulle Caillat. Her browned-butter, press-in tart crust is rightfully legendary—it's a buttery, delicately tender shell that comes together in 20 mostly passive minutes. I've made it countless times, and in trying out lots of other no-roll, press-in crusts, I still return to it because you get a tender, buttery crust, rather than a stiff, dry cracker. I've tinkered with it over time by transferring the cooking to the stovetop, and giving it some nuttiness with whole-wheat flour, which complements savory fillings so nicely. Here, if you aren't using your scale to measure the flour, it's extra important to spoon then level it—too much flour in this tart will yield a crust that cracks. Given the saltiness of the cheese in the filling, my favorite contrasting addition is a sweet-tart jam, swirled to create a marbled effect. But you can also nix the jam, and once baked, arrange blanched spring vegetables, lightly dressed tender greens, thin slices of caramelized squash, or juicy corn kernels and cherry tomatoes over the tart just before serving.

Serves 6 to 8

Crust	Filling
1 stick (4 ounces) butter	8 ounces feta cheese, packed in brine
1 tablespoon neutral-tasting oil,	1 egg
such as grapeseed or avocado oil	¼ teaspoon kosher salt
¼ cup water	Freshly ground black pepper
1 tablespoon sugar	1 to 2 tablespoons milk (optional)
¼ teaspoon kosher salt	2 to 3 tablespoons tart jam or Onion
1 cup (130 grams) all-purpose flour	Jam (page 90)
½ cup (65 grams) whole-wheat flour	

Preheat the oven to 400°F.

First prepare the crust. In a medium saucepan, combine the butter, oil, water, sugar, and salt and set over medium heat. As the butter melts, it'll bubble and foam. Whisk occasionally, allowing the milk solids to brown. While it's simmering, stir together the flours in a bowl. After 8 to 10 minutes, the butter mixture will thicken slightly and turn a deeper shade of golden, and the bubbles will appear clearer and less foamy—remove it from the heat. Immediately add the flours to the saucepan and stir with a wooden spoon or spatula until a pasty dough forms.

Scrape the mixture into a 9- or 9½-inch tart shell or springform pan, and let it cool for a few minutes until it's safe to touch. Use your fingers to press in the dough so that it's evenly distributed across the bottom and sides of the pan (if using a springform pan, press the dough about

(cont.)

¾ inch up the sides, making the rim as even as possible). Prick the dough with the tines of a fork, then press the fork against the sides to create a ruffled edge. Transfer to the oven and bake for 8 to 12 minutes, until lightly browned. Cool for 5 minutes.

Meanwhile, prepare the filling. In a food processor, process the cheese until smooth. Add the egg, salt, and pepper, and process again. The mixture should be loose enough to pour, about the consistency of pancake batter. If necessary, blend in 1 to 2 tablespoons milk to thin it out. Scrape in to the prebaked crust. (It'll be a fairly thin layer, but it's very rich and flavorful.) Dollop your addition of choice over the surface, then use a small knife to swirl it into the cheese filling.

Reduce the oven temperature to 300°F, then bake the tart for 14 to 18 minutes, until just set in the center. Cool for at least 15 minutes before unmolding and slicing. You can serve the tart warm or at room temperature. It's best on the day it's made, but covered with a piece of plastic wrap and stored in the fridge, it'll keep for up to 2 days. The cheese filling will soften as it comes to room temperature.

AUSTRALIAN ZUCCHINI SLICE

My husband, Vincent, is Australian, and the first time I went to Sydney with him I was captivated by a category of food called "slices." They're what Americans would call bar cookies or iced sheet cakes cut into narrow rectangles, or savory quiche or frittata-like squares. I find the terminology wonderfully appealing, conjuring in my mind a handheld, two- or three-bite affair. As part of his family's Christmas lunch spread, there were little squares of baked egg and zucchini, which I soon learned was the zucchini slice, something Vincent and most of his friends had grown up eating. It's rich, with eggs, and cheese, similar to a frittata cooked in a baking pan but with the addition of flour, which gives it a sturdier texture, somewhere between quiche and a savory muffin.

Makes one 8-by-8-inch pan, enough to serve 8

$1/3$ cup plus 1 tablespoon olive oil, divided	Several grinds black pepper
1 large leek, white and pale green parts only, thinly sliced, or 1 medium onion, diced	5 eggs
	12 to 14 ounces zucchini (2 small or 1 medium), grated
$1\frac{1}{4}$ teaspoon kosher salt, divided	$1/4$ cup Parmesan cheese, grated on a microplane, or $1/2$ cup coarsely grated cheddar
3 cloves garlic, minced	
$1/4$ cup pungent green olives, pitted and finely chopped	1 cup (130 grams) all-purpose flour
	$1\frac{1}{2}$ teaspoon baking powder

Preheat the oven to 350°F. Brush an 8-by-8-inch (2-quart) baking dish with olive oil, then line with a long strip of parchment paper, leaving plenty of overhang on the sides.

In a medium skillet, warm 1 tablespoon of the olive oil over medium heat. Add the leek or onion and $1/4$ teaspoon salt, and cook until softened and beginning to caramelize, 8 to 10 minutes. Stir in the garlic and olives, and cook for another minute or two. Season with black pepper, then set aside to cool slightly as you prepare the rest of the recipe.

In a mixing bowl, whisk the remaining $1/3$ cup oil and eggs together until combined. Stir in the zucchini, the cheese, and the leek mixture. Either sift the flour, baking powder, and remaining 1 teaspoon salt over the wet ingredients, or whisk them together in a small mixing bowl, then add to the egg mixture. Fold until smooth.

Scrape the mixture into the prepared pan and bake until set in the center and lightly browned—this has a moist crumb, so a tester may not come out clean. For a metal pan start checking after 30 minutes, but for a glass or earthenware dish, allow 45 to 55 minutes. It will be puffed up and set in the center when you take it out of the oven, but will sink into an even layer as it cools. Serve warm, room temperature, or chilled.

FARINATA (OR SOCCA) WITH CHICORIES

Chickpea pancakes—based on farinata or socca methods, from Northern Italy or Southern France, respectively—have been such a boon to vegan breakfasts, since they can take on a custardy texture and somewhat eggy flavor. But when made traditionally, which is to say *thin* and crispy, there's not really any need to reframe them as a plant-based substitute. They're so light and flaky and scrumptious; they're as addictive to eat as French fries, and make sense as a popular street food item. I find radicchio to be a terrific vegetable topping, adding some smokiness as it chars in the hot oven, as well as some succulent texture that doesn't interfere with the texture of the farinata. And I learned the wonderful tip of pouring the batter over an upside-down spoon into the pan from Enrica Monzani's terrific blog *A Small Kitchen in Genoa*, which ensures that the batter spreads over the hot oil rather than puncturing the surface (and later sticking to the pan). You may want to double or triple the recipe and cook them off to order, as they won't last long at the table.

Makes one 10-inch farinata, to serve 3 or 4

½ cup plus 2 tablespoons (70 grams) chickpea flour	2 tablespoons olive oil, plus extra for drizzling
¾ cup water	Handful chopped radicchio
Scant ½ teaspoon kosher salt	Freshly ground black pepper
	Flaky salt

Put the chickpea flour in a mixing bowl, then whisk in the water a little at a time to break up all the lumps. The mixture should be a slightly thinner than traditional pancake batter, but a little thicker than heavy cream. Cover and let stand at room temperature for at least 2 hours, and up to 8.

Preheat the oven to 450°F. If you have a baking stone or steel, place it on a rack in the lower third of the oven, and set your cast-iron skillet on top of it to preheat as well. Leave it in there for at least 20 minutes to fully heat up.

Carefully remove the skillet from the oven. Whisk the salt into the batter. Add the olive oil to the hot skillet, swirling gently to cover the base. Flip a serving spoon upside down and angle it in the center of the skillet, and pour the batter so that it hits the spoon and fans across the pan over the warm oil. Scatter the radicchio over the top and transfer to the oven. Bake for 18 to 22 minutes, until lightly blistered on top, browned along the edges, and set in the center.

Allow to cool for a few minutes, then slide onto a cutting board and cut into irregular wedges. Sprinkle with flaky salt and pepper, drizzle with a bit of extra olive oil, then serve while warm.

HERBY SEASONING BLENDS FOR BOILED EGGS + AVOCADO WEDGES

These seasoning blends give a simple boiled egg or wedge of avocado effortless personality, creating a distinctively dressed-up, hearty option on the snack plate. But the fact is, once you've got a home-made seasoned salt on hand, it becomes a flavor block for almost anything you're cooking. I like to keep mine in a little bowl right next to my salt and pepper, and this way I'm always reminded to sprinkle them over salads, scrambled eggs, soup, warm beans, roasted vegetables, bowls of rice, popcorn, and more. These blends all center on fresh herbs, which you'll dry yourself. While you can dry them over a day or two in a draft-free spot, or even inside your oven overnight where the pilot light generates some warmth, I almost always speed things along by cooking them at the lowest temperature my toaster oven allows.

Cumin-Oregano Salt | Makes about 1 tablespoon

If you don't have a mortar and pestle, carefully mince some of the seeds using a chef's knife to crack them open—but whole seeds in the finished salt blend are great, too, because they create a nice texture.

---

6 to 8 bushy oregano sprigs
1 teaspoon cumin seeds

1 teaspoon coarse or flaky salt

Preheat your oven or toaster oven to 225°F (or as low a temperature as it will allow). Line a small baking sheet with parchment paper and arrange the oregano sprigs on it. Bake for about 30 minutes, until the oregano is completely dried out and crisp. Cool, then gently rub the leaves with your fingers until they all come off the stems, and discard the stems. Meanwhile, toast the cumin seeds in a small skillet over medium-low heat until fragrant, swirling often, 3 to 5 minutes, then cool slightly. Pound them coarsely in a mortar and pestle, then mix with the oregano and salt, using your hands to crush the leaves and salt crystals together. Dump the mixture onto a piece of parchment paper and use it as a chute to slide it into a jar or bowl.

(cont.)

Orange + Thyme Salt | Makes about 1 tablespoon

Here's an incredibly fragrant blend—especially good sprinkled over popcorn, as well as almost any kind of roasted vegetable.

Zest of 1 orange	1 teaspoon coarse or flaky salt
6 to 8 bushy sprigs thyme	¼ teaspoon ground black pepper

Preheat your oven or toaster oven to 225°F (or as low a temperature as it will allow). Line a small baking sheet with parchment paper and use a rasp-style grater to zest the orange over one half of the sheet. Set the thyme sprigs on the other side and transfer to the oven. Bake for about 20 minutes, stirring the zest every 5 minutes to help it evenly dry out, until both the zest and thyme are dry. Allow to cool, then rub the thyme leaves off their stems, right on the parchment, and pick out the stems. Use the paper as a chute to transfer the zest and thyme to a bowl, and combine with the salt and pepper by mixing with your fingers. To transfer the salt blend to a container, dump it back on the parchment paper, then use it as a chute again to slide it into a jar or bowl.

Coriander, Fennel + Celery Salt | Makes about 2 tablespoons

Look for a head of celery that you can tell has leaves still attached, though there will likely be plenty of leaves surrounding the celery heart. This is an incredibly fragrant seasoning blend, wonderful on creamy things like soft cheese and scrambled eggs, but also great sprinkled over a platter of crudités.

About ½ cup gently packed celery leaves	1 teaspoon coriander seeds
1 teaspoon fennel seeds	1½ teaspoons coarse or flaky salt

Preheat your oven or toaster oven to 225°F (or as low a temperature as it will allow). Line a small baking sheet with parchment paper and spread the leaves out on it in a single layer. Bake for about 20 minutes, stirring after 10 minutes, until the leaves shrink and begin to dry out. Allow to cool, during which time they'll become more crisp. Meanwhile, toast the fennel seeds in a small skillet over medium-low heat until fragrant, swirling often, 3 to 5 minutes, then cool and add to a mortar along with the coriander seeds and salt. Pound to coarsely break up the seeds. Using the parchment paper as a chute, transfer the celery leaves to the mortar and use your hands to crunch up the leaves and incorporate them into the salt. To transfer the salt blend to a container, dump it back on the parchment paper, then use it as a chute again to slide it into a jar or bowl.

Rosemary, Lemon + Chili Salt | Makes about 2 tablespoons

Baking this blended salt briefly speeds up the dehydration, but it will also dry out on its own if spread over a plate or platter and left at room temperature for a day.

1 tablespoon minced rosemary	½ teaspoon mild dried chili
Zest of 1 lemon	1 tablespoon coarse or flaky salt

Preheat your oven or toaster oven to 225°F (or as low a temperature as it will allow) and line a small baking sheet with parchment paper. Combine all ingredients in a small bowl, mixing with your fingers to coax out oils, then spread on a small baking sheet. Transfer to the oven and bake for about 10 minutes, then leave in the oven to cool—at least 30 minutes. Once the rosemary is dry, use the parchment paper as a chute to transfer the seasoning to a bowl or small jar.

Perfect Boiled Eggs

If you're wanting a yolk that's vibrant in color and has a creamy, fudgy texture, here's how to do it. I often batch these so that I have them on hand for snacking over the span of a few days, but a just-cooked, still-warm boiled egg is a wonderful treat you shouldn't deprive yourself of.

4 eggs

Fill a medium saucepan with water and bring to boil. Using a slotted spoon (or a spider skimmer, or tongs), gently add the eggs to the water. Once it returns to a boil, reduce the heat to a gentle simmer and cook for 8 minutes. Lift them out of the water with the slotted spoon and transfer to an ice bath or, when aiming to serve them while still warm, peel the eggs under running cold water. Once cool, the cooked eggs will keep for at least 3 days stored in the refrigerator.

SPINACH + RICOTTA DIP, À LA SAAG PANEER

This warm spinach dip is a slight reworking of the North Indian dish saag paneer, and it's shaped by the version I was introduced to by Rohan Kamicheril on his blog *The Tiffin Club*. His recipe isn't enriched with cream, but instead is a gorgeously pure expression of good spinach, which is sweet and velvety in texture when in season. I then dollop fresh ricotta over the warm dip, which lends it necessary creaminess. Serve with pita chips or warmed flatbreads, using melted ghee for the fat.

Serves 4 to 6

10 ounces spinach, fresh or frozen
2 tablespoons ghee or butter
1 teaspoon cumin seeds
½ onion, finely diced
½ teaspoon kosher salt, plus additional
   to taste
3 cloves garlic, minced
1 tablespoon finely grated ginger

1 or 2 Indian green chiles (or bird's eye,
   or serrano), minced
1 teaspoon ground coriander
1 teaspoon garam masala
1 cup water
½ cup fresh ricotta
Cilantro leaves, for garnish
Lemon wedges, for serving

If using fresh spinach: Add about a ¼ inch of water to a medium skillet and bring it to a simmer. Then pile in the spinach, adding it incrementally as it cooks down, and stirring frequently, until the spinach is cooked down and bright green. Transfer to a colander to cool until safe to handle, then squeeze out excess liquid and finely chop.

If using frozen spinach: Fill a medium saucepan with water and bring to a boil. Add the spinach, and when the water comes back to boil, it should be fully thawed. Strain through a fine-mesh sieve and cool until safe to handle, then squeeze out the excess liquid and finely chop.

Melt the ghee in an oven-safe, medium skillet over medium heat, then add the cumin seeds, stirring until fragrant. Add the onion and the salt, and cook until it begins to caramelize, about 6 to 10 minutes.

Mince the garlic, ginger, and green chili (seeding the chili if desired) together on your cutting board with a pinch of salt, until it resembles a coarse paste. Add to the onions once they've begun to caramelize.

Stir in the spinach until well combined, followed by the coriander and garam masala, then add the water. Bring to a simmer, then partially cover the skillet and continue cooking for about 10 minutes over low heat, until the mixture has darkened a shade and the liquid has reduced. Transfer to a blender, or a tall container that fits a handheld immersion blender, and puree. Return it to the skillet to rewarm. Either dollop the ricotta over the spinach and serve directly out of the skillet, or transfer it to a serving bowl and garnish with the cheese, cilantro, and lemon wedges. Serve hot or warm.

CHEWY-CRISPY TOFU STICKS WITH CHILI-GINGER JAM DIPPING SAUCE

These little morsels—a sort of crude American adaptation of the deep-fried tofu part of agedashi tofu—really do remind me of mozzarella sticks. And the pleasure is very similar. The breading takes on a bit of both crispiness (thanks to panko bread crumbs) and light chewiness (thanks to potato or cornstarch), and salting both the tofu and the breading is key. Shallow-frying is perfectly fine: you need only a quarter inch of oil or so, and as long as the oil is heated, the crusts will stay light and crispy, and you'll avoid the oil seeping into the food and making it leaden and soggy. I love these with the accompanying Ginger-Chili Jam Dipping Sauce (below), but they welcome all kinds of condiments.

Serves 4 to 6

One 14- to 16-ounce package water-packed firm tofu
Kosher salt
4 tablespoons potato starch or cornstarch

4 tablespoons panko bread crumbs
Neutral-tasting oil (grapeseed or avocado oil), for frying
Ginger-Chili Jam Dipping Sauce (recipe follows)

Drain the tofu and gently blot off excess liquid, then slice in half height-wise, like a layer cake. Arrange the two pieces in a single layer on a clean kitchen towel, then fold over the towel's excess. Set a cutting board and something heavy on top and continue to drain for at least 15 minutes.

Cut each piece of tofu in half lengthwise, then into sticks about 2 inches long and roughly ½ inch thick. You should have 16 pieces. Sprinkle them lightly and evenly with salt.

In a shallow bowl, stir together the potato starch, bread crumbs, and ½ teaspoon salt. Pour oil into a heavy skillet or wok to a depth of ¼ inch, and warm over medium heat. Working in batches, dredge the tofu pieces through the dry mixture, coating them well on all sides.

Test the oil temperature by dipping a corner of a tofu piece into the pan. It should sizzle immediately. Fry the pieces in batches—as many as will fit in a loose single layer—until crisp and lightly golden brown all over, 5 to 7 minutes, turning them as necessary to fry evenly on all sides. Reduce the heat if necessary, to prevent over-browning. Drain briefly then serve warm, with the Chili-Ginger Jam Dipping Sauce.

Chili-Ginger Jam Dipping Sauce

In a small saucepan, combine one 14.5 ounce can of crushed tomatoes, ¼ cup of Chili-Ginger Jam (page 91, or any store-bought pepper jelly), and 2 tablespoons olive oil, and bring to a simmer. Cook for 15 minutes, then season with salt to taste.

SAVORY PEAR TART

A package of frozen puff pastry always reminds me of my mom, and how she used it so often for many of her favorite warm and gooey appetizers. I've been making a version of this tart for years. It began with apples and had a cheese component, but it's since gone more in the direction of pissaladière (a French onion tart), with a thin smear of Dijon mustard beneath caramelized shallots and the fruit. There are some terrific all-butter brands of puff pastry that are widely available (I like Dufour), and while the Pepperidge Farm brand is heavily processed, it's vegan, which means that this can be an easy vegan dish as well.

Serves 8 to 10

3 medium, firm pears (Bosc, Bartlett, Anjou, or Forelle)	One store-bought package puff pastry (10 to 14 ounces), thawed per package instructions
2 tablespoons butter or olive oil	2 heaping tablespoons Dijon mustard
4 medium shallots, sliced into ¼-inch strips	1 teaspoon fresh thyme leaves
Kosher salt	Freshly ground black pepper

Preheat the oven to 450°F. Line a baking sheet with parchment paper. Arrange an oven rack in the bottom third of your oven, and place another one in the top third.

Cut the pears into ½-inch-thick wedges: Slice them in half through the stem, then carefully trim out the core. With each half lying flat on the cutting board, cut into wedges.

Melt the butter or warm the olive oil over medium heat, then add the shallots and a few pinches of salt. Cook until they begin to take on some color, 6 to 8 minutes, then stir in the pears. Cook the pears until they begin to soften and the contents of the pan start to thicken slightly, 10 to 15 minutes. Remove from the heat and cool.

On a lightly floured surface, roll out the puff pastry sheet into a rectangle roughly the size of your baking sheet. Some brands are thicker than others—this is a flexible tart, so any rustic rectangle will work great. Fold the dough over your rolling pin and unfurl it onto the prepared baking sheet. Use a sharp knife to trace a border around the dough about ½ inch from the edge of the sheet, cutting into the dough but not all the way through it. Dollop the mustard over the surface and spread it evenly within that border (a small offset spatula works great for this), then spread the pear-and-shallot mixture over the mustard layer. Sprinkle the thyme on top as well as a few grinds of black pepper. Fold the ½-inch border over the edge of the filling.

Bake on the lower rack of your oven for 15 minutes, then transfer to the upper rack. Cook until the crust is well browned, 20 to 30 minutes. Serve warm or at room temperature, sliced into rectangles or squares.

CABBAGE + TOMATO TART IN YEASTED WHOLE-WHEAT SHELL

One of my top influences is Martha Rose Shulman, whose long-running Recipes for Health column in the *New York Times* always hit the perfect nexus of being healthy, approachable, technically exciting, and inventive, but connected to her research, travel, and professional experience. That's where I encountered the concept of a yeasted pastry shell, which in Shulman's hands is enriched with olive oil and bolstered with whole-wheat flour. You wouldn't confuse it for a flaky, buttery, pâte brisée—it's a bit more like a thin, tender pizza crust—but often this is the style of pastry that I want to pair with my vegetable fillings. I've tweaked her recipe to eliminate the egg, which makes this my go-to vegan tart shell. The filling consists simply of a smear of Cultured Cashew Ricotta (page 89), and a pile of softened cabbage that concentrates in flavor during its bake in the oven. In the winter, I top the cabbage with halved or thinly sliced store-bought cherry tomatoes, but in the summer, I replace them with slices of juicy, ripe summer tomato.

Serves 6

Pastry

½ cup (65 grams) all-purpose flour

½ cup (60 grams) whole-wheat pastry flour

1 teaspoon instant yeast (preferably Saf-Instant)

¼ teaspoon kosher salt

Pinch of sugar

¼ cup warm water

2½ tablespoons olive oil, plus additional for brushing

Filling

2 tablespoons olive oil

3 cups shredded green cabbage (about 6 ounces, or ½ small-medium head)

Kosher salt

¼ cup white wine

2 teaspoons all-purpose flour

Freshly ground black pepper

½ cup Cultured Cashew Ricotta (page 89) or Fresh Ricotta (page 87)

½ cup sliced cherry tomatoes or 1 medium, ripe sliced tomato

(cont.)

To prepare the pastry: Whisk together the flours, yeast, salt, and sugar. Drizzle the water and oil over the mixture, and then use a wooden spoon or spatula to combine, stirring until a mass forms. Use your hands to knead the mixture for a few minutes, until a smooth dough forms. Shape into a ball. Wipe the mixing bowl clean and lightly oil it, then return the dough to the bowl. Cover and allow to rise until doubled, about an hour.

Meanwhile, warm the remaining 2 tablespoons of olive oil in a medium skillet over medium-high heat, then add the cabbage and a big pinch of salt, stirring to coat. Add the wine, then cover the pan and cook until very tender, about 10 to 12 minutes. Remove the lid and stir in the 2 teaspoons of flour. Cook for a few minutes more, until the pan appears dry, then remove from the heat. Season with salt and pepper to taste. Allow to cool.

Preheat the oven to 375°F, and line a baking sheet with parchment paper. Sprinkle the tomatoes with a few pinches of salt and lay out on paper towels to drain for at least 10 minutes.

Dust a work surface lightly with flour, then transfer the risen dough to it. Roll it into a thin circle about 12 inches in diameter. Transfer to the prepared baking sheet. Spread the cashew cheese over the dough, leaving a 1-inch border, then pile the cabbage on top of it. Arrange the tomatoes over the top, then fold the exposed border over the filling, pleating as you go. Brush the crust lightly with olive oil.

Bake for 30 to 40 minutes, until the crust is lightly golden brown. Serve warm or at room temperature.

VEGETARIAN HAND ROLLS (TEMAKI SUSHI)

One of Vincent's and my favorite "snack spots" is Daigo Hand Roll Bar, at the Dekalb Market Hall in downtown Brooklyn. Per its name, Daigo's specialty is a thoughtful, impeccably made menu of Japanese temaki sushi, a style where rice and sushi fillings are rolled up like a cigar in a piece of toasted nori, handed over directly by the chef, and meant to be eaten immediately—before the nori loses its crispness and the delicate balance of temperatures (warm rice, cool fillings) escapes its ideal window. It's probably the most pleasurable eating experience either of us has ever had while standing up. While making this style of sushi at home pales in comparison to the craft on display at Daigo, it's nonetheless a delicious and interactive snacks-for-dinner meal. You can prep an assortment of fillings in advance, and then let everyone at the dinner table assemble as they please. Take care when seasoning your rice, stirring it gently when you add the vinegar to prevent it from getting mushy. And get creative with the fillings—it's a fun opportunity to dig out lingering condiments and leftovers from the back of your fridge. But, as with the rice, spend some time preparing them. This temaki is meant to be eaten straight out of hand, and the fillings should be prepped in a way that makes them easy to bite through without creating any mess. To that end, avoid the temptation to overfill them. Each roll is a three- or four-bite snack.

Sushi Rice

1½ cups short-grain Japanese sushi rice
1½ cups water
One 2-by-2-inch square kombu

3 tablespoons rice vinegar
½ teaspoon kosher salt
¼ teaspoon sugar

For Assembly and Serving

6 sheets untoasted nori
Soy sauce

Wasabi paste

Filling Suggestions

Cucumbers, sliced into thin
  matchsticks
Avocado, sliced into thin wedges
Kimchi, coarsely chopped
Mango, sliced into thin matchsticks
Purple or daikon radish, sliced into thin
  matchsticks
Crunchy sprouts, such as sunflower
  sprouts

Pickled Shiitake Mushrooms (recipe
  below)
Baked Japanese "Omelet," sliced into
  thin strips (recipe below)
Citrus Carrots (page 60), sliced into
  matchsticks
Gingery Quick-Pickled Beets (page 64),
  sliced into matchsticks

(cont.)

Kohlrabi

Baked Japanese "Omelet" (p. 138)

Soy Sauce

Pickled Shiitake Mushrooms (p. 139)

Toasted Nori

Citrus Carrots (p. 60)

Cucumber

Kimchi

Gingery
Quick-
Pickled Beets
(p. 64)

Sprouts

To make the rice: Place the rice in a bowl or saucepan and cover with an inch of water. Swish the grains gently a few times, then drain off the water. Repeat twice. The idea here is to rinse off excess starch from the grains. Then combine the drained rice with 1½ cups of water, either in the saucepan you plan to cook it in, or the bowl that fits into your rice cooker, and soak for at least 30 minutes.

If using a rice cooker to cook your rice—add the kombu to the rice and water, and simply follow the manufacturer's instructions for cooking white rice. Or, to cook on the stovetop, add the kombu to the rice and place over medium-high heat to bring the water to a boil. Once it comes to a boil and the water level has dipped down to the level of the rice, cover the pan, reduce the heat to its lowest setting, and cook for 18 minutes. Remove from the heat and let stand for 10 minutes more.

Meanwhile, whisk together the rice vinegar, salt, and sugar in a small bowl, until the solids dissolve.

Transfer the rice to a wide mixing bowl, a handai (which is the traditional wooden rice bowl), or a wooden salad bowl, which is what I use. Drizzle the seasoned vinegar over the rice as evenly as you can, then gently fold the rice to distribute the seasonings, resisting the urge to mash the rice by folding too aggressively. If using a rice cooker, return the rice into it and keep on the warm setting. If cooking on the stovetop, return the rice to the saucepan and cover with a lid to keep warm.

Cut the nori sheets in half using scissors, creating two long rectangles from each.

When you're ready to serve, toast each nori sheet by briefly waving it over your stovetop burner set to medium-high, until it becomes fragrant and crispens slightly. This will only take a few seconds. Stack the sheets as you go, taking care to not let them get wet.

With a toasted nori sheet flat on your work surface, spread about 2 tablespoons of rice into an even layer that covers about half of it in a square shape. Arrange desired fillings on top, then roll up like a cigar and eat immediately.

Baked Japanese "Omelet" | Makes one 8-by-8-inch omelet

The rolled Japanese omelet called tamagoyaki is made by cooking thin layers of beaten egg, dashi, and other flavorings in a square-shaped skillet and, as each layer cooks, rolling it up into a cigar, and then continuing to add more small amounts of egg, layer by layer, rolling each one over the next, until you've got a thick omelet in which all the individual layers are visible when you cut it crosswise. It's a fun thing to make, and you can even do it in a round skillet. But for hand rolls, where the omelet is meant to be a filling rather than a standalone item, I've simplified the process by cooking the dashi-seasoned eggs in a single thin layer in a square pan in the oven. This also makes it easy to portion out and size into strips that are perfect for the hand rolls.

1 strip kombu	4 eggs
2 cups water	1 tablespoon sugar
Neutrally flavored oil, such as	1 teaspoon mirin
grapeseed, canola, or vegetable	¼ teaspoon kosher salt

First, make the dashi: Combine the kombu and water in a saucepan and bring to a bare simmer—don't let it boil. Fish out the kombu, and set mixture aside to cool until warm.

Preheat the oven to 350°F. Brush an 8-by-8-inch square baking pan liberally with oil, then line with two long overlapping strips of parchment paper, allowing overhang on the ends.

Beat the eggs thoroughly, then whisk in ¼ cup of the kombu dashi (save the remaining for soup or sipping), as well as the sugar, mirin, and salt. Pour the mixture into the prepared pan and transfer to the oven. Bake until the eggs are just set, 14 to 18 minutes. Cool until warm, then use the parchment paper overhang to lift the egg from the pan. Slice into long, narrow strips the same length as your nori squares above.

Pickled Shiitake Mushrooms | Makes about 1 cup

Dried shiitake mushrooms are such a valuable part of the vegetarian kitchen. Reconstituted in warm water, they have a much stronger flavor than their fresh counterpart. Here they're reconstituted, and then covered in a flavorful marinade. In the hand rolls, they add meaty texture and deep flavor, but these are an equally useful thing to have on hand to dress up grain bowls, salads, sandwiches, and the like.

1 cup whole dried shiitake mushrooms	¹/₃ cup sherry, rice, or apple cider
¹/₃ cup soy sauce	vinegar
	3 tablespoons honey
	¼ teaspoon kosher salt

Place the dried mushrooms in a small saucepan and cover with water. Bring to a simmer, then remove from the heat and allow to steep for 10 to 15 minutes, until fully reconstituted. Slice a mushroom in half to check for sure—they should be softened all the way through. Strain off the water, then, when safe to handle, trim off and discard the mushroom stems and slice the caps into thin strips. Transfer the sliced caps into a heat-safe jar or container.

Back in the saucepan, combine the remaining ingredients and place over medium heat. Once the solids are dissolved, remove from the heat and pour over the mushrooms. Once cool, store in the refrigerator for up to a week.

OATMEAL ARANCINI

Since 2018, I've been doing an annual oatmeal challenge called #28daysofoatmeal on Instagram each February, where for each day of the month I share a different way to serve up your daily oats (spoiler: oatmeal, if you like it savory, is a terrific vessel for your leftovers). This has resulted in cooking a lot of steel-cut oats, and these arancini came about from frequently having leftover oatmeal in the fridge and noting that it gels up when it cools in a similar way that leftover risotto does. I don't often make oatmeal specifically for the arancini; it's more often that the leftovers can be brilliantly put to use like this. Cooking the oats in half milk and half water roughly mimics the arancini style of combining the risotto with bechamel to create a creamier consistency in the grains. While you *can* take all kinds of liberties with your fillings, I focus on cheese here, because it's so easy and plays to the subtle nuttiness of the oats. One note: You can't make these with rolled or quick-cooking oats; it's got to be the steel-cut ones.

Makes 10

For the Oatmeal

1 teaspoon olive oil or butter	2 cups water
1 cup steel-cut oats	2 cups whole milk
	½ teaspoon kosher salt

For the Arancini

1 cup all-purpose flour	Freshly ground black pepper
1 egg	Ten ½-inch cubes nicely melting
1 cup fine bread crumbs (see page 221)	cheese, such as mozzarella or fontina
Kosher salt	Olive oil, for frying

In a medium saucepan, warm the olive oil or butter over medium heat, then add the oats and toast them for a few minutes, swirling the pan often, until fragrant and darkened a shade. Pour in the water and milk and bring to a simmer. Stir in the salt, then partially cover the pan, lower the heat to achieve a gentle simmer, and cook for about 20 minutes, until the oats are tender and the mixture is thick. Cool, scrape into an airtight container, and refrigerate overnight. If you're in a rush, you can spread the oatmeal out on a baking sheet and cool it down in the refrigerator for an hour, but they'll thicken best, and be easiest to work with, if chilled overnight.

    When you're ready to make the arancini, create a little assembly station: Place the flour, egg, and bread crumbs in separate shallow bowls. Season each of the three bowls with a pinch of salt and pepper, and whisk the egg until it's an even consistency.

Scoop a heaping tablespoon of oatmeal into the palm of your hand, flattening it out slightly, and place a cheese cube in its center. Take another similarly sized spoonful of oats and sandwich it on top. Then cup the oatmeal between both your hands and shape it into a ball about 2 inches in diameter. Repeat with the remaining oats, arranging them on a small baking sheet or plate as you go.

In a medium saucepan or Dutch oven—something with high walls to protect against splatter—heat about ¾ inch of olive oil. You want to bring it to 375°F, and if you don't have an instant-read thermometer, leave the oil to simmer for about 10 minutes over medium heat. You can test its temperature by dropping in a little dab of oatmeal: if it doesn't sizzle immediately, it needs more time.

Meanwhile, dredge each of the rolled arancini through the flour, then egg, then bread crumbs. Be sure to coat thoroughly, but also be sure to shake off the excess at each stage. It helps to dedicate one hand to the dipping and breading, while keeping the other one dry and clean. Arrange the breaded arancini back on the plate.

Once the oil is hot, add the breaded arancini to the oil in batches of 3 (to avoid dramatically lowering the temperature of the oil) and shallow-fry them until browned all over, turning often, 6 to 8 minutes. Transfer to a cooling rack set over a baking sheet to drain and let cool for a few minutes before eating.

Reheat leftover arancini in a preheated 350°F oven for 10 to 15 minutes.

SQUASH-SUNFLOWER SLIDERS

Sliders are a great format for veggie burgers because there's no need to achieve a burger-like texture. When it's just a two-bite affair, it matters less if their structure doesn't withstand repeated chomping between buns. This mixture has a moist texture that browns nicely and firms up, especially as they cool, and I love the clean flavor of the sunflower seeds, reminiscent of fresh garbanzo beans. Combining the cooking of the squash and quinoa into one pot also simplifies the cleanup a bit and entirely eliminates the need to turn on your oven. They're good enough to serve on their own, sans buns, though the Green Chili + Sunflower Seed Romesco on page 34 is an excellent pairing.

Makes about 16 sliders

½ cup quinoa, rinsed

¾ cup water

8 ounces butternut squash (about ¼ of 1 medium squash), seeded, peeled, and cubed in 1- to 2-inch pieces

1 tablespoon olive oil

2 medium shallots, 1 leek, or 1 medium onion, diced

½ teaspoon kosher salt, plus an additional pinch

1 cup toasted sunflower seeds

1 tablespoon cornstarch, potato starch, or arrowroot

Add the quinoa to a saucepan, along with 1 cup water, and arrange the squash pieces on top. Place over medium-high heat, and when the water begins bubbling, cover the pan and reduce the heat to low. Cook until the quinoa has absorbed the liquid and its germ is exposed, and the squash is tender, 20 to 25 minutes.

Place a skillet over medium heat and add the olive oil. Once warmed, add the shallots and a pinch of salt, and cook until softened, 6 to 8 minutes. Scrape them into the food processor bowl along with the sunflower seeds. Pulse the mixture just until it begins to cohere. Pick out the squash pieces from the quinoa and add them to the food processor along with the ½ teaspoon salt and cornstarch and continue pulsing, integrating the squash with the seed mixture, scraping down the sides a few times. Last, add the cooked quinoa and pulse until combined.

Shape the mixture into patties about 1½ inches wide and ½ inch thick. Warm a thin film of olive oil in a skillet over medium heat. Working in batches, cook the sliders on each side for 3 to 4 minutes, until lightly browned and warmed through. Add more oil to the pan as needed. Serve warm or at room temperature. In an airtight container in the refrigerator, they'll keep for up to 3 days.

SLIDER TOPPINGS

Umami Roasted Tomatoes (p. 63)

Honeyed Pickled Shallots (p. 62)

Stovetop Maple-Ale Mustard (p. 100)

Citrus Carrots (p. 60)

Pure Green Soup (p. 168)

Vegan Spinach + Cheese Pierogi (p. 145)

VEGAN SPINACH + CHEESE PIEROGI

When I moved to New York in 2002, I landed in Greenpoint, Brooklyn, which was (and still is) a neighborhood with deep Polish roots, and that's where I first encountered pierogi, those substantial, pillowy dumplings that so often come with a plop of sour cream and a spoonful of soft, oily caramelized onions. I ate many of them, most often as an inexpensive snack, but didn't consider making my own until I recently stumbled on Michal Korkosz's terrific book, *Fresh from Poland*, where he puts the focus squarely on Poland's local and vegetable-centric food traditions. From him and other cooks, I learned that pierogi dough is a matter of personal preference. Many enrich their dough with eggs or oil (or both), while for others it's just flour and water; like Michal, I find the oil-based dough yields the best results and is most satisfying to work with. Approach this recipe as a project—a rewarding one. You can prepare the filling a day or two in advance, but you'll need to make the pierogi dough the same day you assemble them. (Enlist some friends for assembly!) Folding the pierogi, in my experience, is trickier than other similar types of dumplings, because you want them packed to the brim with filling, or else they end up being doughy. It takes a little practice, but remember that regardless of what they look like, they'll be delicious. And feel free to use non-vegan farmers' cheese or ricotta here if you like.

Makes about 40 dumplings

Filling

8 ounces Yukon Gold potato (about 2 medium), peeled and diced

Olive oil

5 ounces fresh or frozen spinach (about 5 cups fresh)

½ large or 1 small white or yellow onion, diced

Kosher salt

½ cup Cultured Cashew Ricotta (page 89), or store-bought alternative

Freshly ground black pepper

A few swipes of freshly grated nutmeg, using a rasp-style grater

Pierogi Dough

3 cups (390 grams) all-purpose flour

¾ teaspoon kosher salt

¾ cup hot tap water

3 tablespoons good olive oil

For Serving

Good olive oil

Flaky salt

Freshly ground black pepper

(cont.)

To make the filling: Fill a medium saucepan with ½ inch water and fit with a steamer insert. Bring the water to a boil, then add the potato, cover, and cook until the potato is tender and falls off a paring knife when pierced, about 8 to 10 minutes. Uncover and remove from the heat.

If using fresh spinach: Warm a splash of olive oil in a medium skillet over medium heat, then add the spinach and cook, stirring with tongs, until wilted. Transfer to a plate or cutting board or colander. When cooled until safe to handle, squeeze out as much liquid as you can and coarsely chop.

If using frozen spinach: Bring a saucepan full of water to boil, then add the spinach (straight out of the freezer; no need to thaw). Cover the pan, and once the water comes back to a boil, the spinach should be thawed. Pour through a sieve. Rinse under cold running water, then squeeze dry, and coarsely chop.

Return the pan to the heat and warm 2 tablespoons olive oil in a medium skillet over medium heat, then add the onion and ½ teaspoon salt. Cook, stirring often, until the onion becomes golden and sweet, 10 to 15 minutes. Stir in the spinach, then remove from the heat. Add the potato to the pan and use a fork to mash it thoroughly into the mixture, then stir in the cheese, a few grinds of black pepper, and the nutmeg. Taste, adjusting seasonings as necessary. Transfer to a bowl and keep it in the fridge as you prepare the pierogi dough. Stored in an airtight container, you can make the filling up to 2 days in advance.

To make the pierogi dough: In a mixing bowl, stir together the flour and salt. In a tall measuring cup, combine the hot water and olive oil. Slowly add the liquids into the dry ingredients bit by bit while mixing the dough, and continue stirring until it becomes a shaggy mass. Transfer the dough to a clean work surface lightly dusted with flour, and knead until it becomes smooth and pliable, adding additional flour as needed to prevent sticking. It should be a moist, slightly tacky dough but not wet or excessively sticky. Wrap tightly or cover with an inverted bowl to prevent it from drying out, and allow to rest for at least 30 minutes, and up to a few hours.

Alternatively, make the dough with a stand mixer: Using the paddle attachment, stir together the flour and salt. In a tall measuring cup, combine the water and olive oil. With the motor running on low speed, pour the liquid into the dry ingredients in a slow, steady stream, and continue mixing until a shaggy mass forms. Switch to the dough hook, and knead the dough until it becomes smooth and pliable, adding additional flour as needed to prevent it from sticking—though some sticking on the bottom of the bowl is normal. Transfer to a piece of plastic or other container to wrap tightly and prevent it from drying out, then rest the dough for at least 30 minutes.

Cut the dough into 3 pieces. Working one at a time (and keeping the other pieces covered with a clean kitchen towel or inverted bowl to prevent drying out), use a rolling pin to roll the dough out to an even thickness of about $1/16$ inch. Use a 2½-inch round biscuit (or pierogi) cutter to cut out as many circles as you can, transfer them to a baking sheet that's been lightly dusted with flour, and keep them covered with a clean towel. Scrape up the trimmings and set them aside. Repeat with remaining pieces of dough, rerolling the scraps as well.

To assemble: Working one at a time, use your hands to gently stretch each round a bit more, until it's between 3 and 3½ inches in diameter. Place about 2 teaspoons of filling in the center, then fold it over and use your hands to seal. This can be tricky, as you want the pierogi to be as filled up as possible. Try to get the cut edges of the dough to touch, then gently pinch the dough to seal from the outside edge, working toward the center, leaving a thin rim. It's a very forgiving dough, so it's not a huge problem if any of the filling ends up on the wrong side of the wrapper as long as you've got a seal. If the dough isn't sealing, moisten your fingers with water as you press. Repeat with remaining dumpling rounds and fillings, arranging the prepared dumplings on a sheet pan, and keeping it covered as you work.

To serve: Bring a pot of water to boil. Add pierogi about 10 at a time—or as many as will fit comfortably in a single layer in your pot—and stir gently to prevent them from sticking to the bottom of the pot. Cover until the water returns to a boil, then remove lid and cook until they rise to the surface. Use a slotted spoon to transfer the pierogi directly to a plate or platter. Drizzle with olive oil, plus salt and pepper, and serve hot.

Freezing instructions: You can freeze the prepared pierogi for up to 3 months. Place a baking sheet, on which they're arranged in a single layer, in the freezer for about 2 hours, until firm, then pack them into a large container or resealable bags. To cook them, add directly from the freezer to a pot of boiling water, and once they rise to the surface, cook for 1 to 2 minutes more.

Snack Box

Focaccia + A Cucumber (v)

Spiced Pistachios (v, gf)

Spicy Walnut-Feta Dip (gf)

Mixed Mushroom Pâté (v, gf)

Almond Cake with Plums (gf)
by Eric Sze of Ursula

xo
Lukas & Vincent

A Snack Box Wedding

In March 2020, Vincent and I got married at the Arch of Reno Walk-In Wedding Chapel, by a man we'd never met named Dave, just a few hours before most of the country went into strict COVID-19 lockdowns. While Reno hadn't been in our original plan—we'd meant to do it at the beautiful and historic City Hall in downtown Manhattan, not too far from the stately entrance to the Brooklyn Bridge—the elopement itself *was* our plan, perhaps because for most of our lives we didn't imagine being able to get married and therefore never put much energy into imagining what kind of a production it'd be. There in Reno, the most iconic nearby landmark was the neon sign marking THE BIGGEST LITTLE CITY IN THE WORLD. Somehow, it felt right. Dave's words were beautiful and sobering, lending gravity to the moment in a way that we honestly weren't expecting. What a joy it was to simply be married. Both everything and nothing had changed between us.

But after spending much of the year distanced, we were yearning to see our friends. And we realized through those months that a traditional wedding may be less about various traditions, and more about getting all one's favorite people into the same place at the same time—such a rarity as everyone gets older and obligations multiply. A delayed wedding celebration would provide the perfect excuse to do just that.

So, seven months after our wedding date, still navigating the eggshells of a social life in 2020 but following the guidance at the time, we chose a warm October Sunday afternoon and a grassy expanse in Brooklyn's Prospect Park, and invited our New York–based friends to come for an unstructured little gathering. There was no schedule, no speech, no ceremony—it was entirely about bringing our friends together. There was just one nonnegotiable: snacks. Specifically, a personal box of them, one for each guest. I could picture it perfectly: a kraft-paper parcel, passed out like gifts for everyone to enjoy from their socially distanced blanket islands, curated with some of our favorite bites, all designed for easy, mess-free eating right out of hand. Leading up to the event, I mapped out a menu and ordered supplies, and the weekend before our celebration, Vincent and I got to work shopping and preparing all the food.

It was crisp and mostly sunny on that Sunday, and we spent the morning pulling the various elements together: folding boxes, wrapping napkins around little wooden knives, printing off snack box menus, and finalizing how we'd arrange everything in the boxes. I baked off My Ideal Focaccia and sliced it up into soldier-style rectangles. We divvied up little cups of Toasted Walnut + Feta Dip, Mixed Mushroom Pâté, and Smoky Glazed Pistachios. We wrapped quarters of Persian cucumber in parchment paper, like pickles, as a crudité, and for a sweet, we enlisted our talented pastry friend Eric See—he came up with an almond cake topped with fresh plums and pistachios. Last, my friend Izzy Forman gifted us a case of bubbly wine from Oyster River Winegrowers, produced from her local vineyard in Maine. It was a full and proper menu—worthy of the occasion.

Along with blankets, cups, a cooler, some bottled fizzy water, and a portable speaker, we loaded the snack boxes into a collapsible wagon, piled high and teetering, and rolled it into the park from our apartment near its southeastern entrance. As our friends trickled in, we immediately realized what an incredible gift it was just to be able to see them. Our being married was something we were eager to share, of course, but in the context of 2020, their physical presence was enough to make us giddy. Some we were able to hug, others not—but regardless, we felt the love emanating. And when my friend Kathryn called for an impromptu speech, the sun broke through the clouds, saturating the moment in syrupy October light that felt blessed. I quietly hoped that at some point in the future, we'd regard the masks dangling over our ears in all the photos with less a feeling of panicked fatigue, and more one of appreciation for the unmistakable timestamp.

It all felt quite full circle. From the Arch of Reno to Prospect Park, there was a united sense of spirit, appropriate, perhaps, for the circumstances and the conditions of a wedding in 2020. Planned somewhat, but we also winged it, and trusting our guts about creating meaning and value on our own terms. In fact, it wasn't entirely unlike the snack boxes themselves, which capture a sense of intention with spontaneity.

And of course they worked out perfectly, hitting all the right notes, with the rich mushroom pâté, tangy-creamy feta, crunchy-spicy pistachios, and crisp cucumber, and no one has ever complained about freshly made focaccia. If you're ever charged with sorting out the food for a wedding, I can't recommend a thoughtful snack box enough.

A Snack Box Wedding Menu

My Ideal Focaccia (page 185)

Smoky Glazed Pistachios (page 40)

Toasted Walnut + Feta Dip (page 83)

Mixed Mushroom Pâté (page 82)

Persian Cucumbers

A Wedding Snack Cake (page 225)

2019 Morphos Pet Nat, by Oyster River Winegrowers

SMALL BUT MIGHTY | SALADS + SOUPS

I love the challenge of turning salads and soups into snacks—it's so unexpected. But what terrific snacks they can be, in large part because they're both so intrinsically designed to center around vegetables. My reworking of these salads involves nudging them in the direction of a Mediterranean-style mezze: everything chopped or shredded into small pieces for salads that are intensely flavored, nutritionally packed, and versatile enough to complement other snacks at the table. And as I found myself reaching for a new utensil to make eating them a bit easier, I even started thinking of them as "spoon salads." The prep sometimes involves creative knife work, breaking down vegetables like asparagus and Brussels sprouts into finer pieces that easily mix with other salad components, which makes them striking at the table. You'll find feathery carrot gratings combined with tender lentils and chewy little bits of dates. Or larger chunks of radishes roasted until just tender, then paired with grapefruit, fried ginger threads, and mint. Or celery, accented with candied little tangles of crispy shallot and almonds. These salads may look small, but they're mighty.

And these little soups are mighty, too. I learned of soup's potential as a snack one summer while I was whipping up yet another batch of cold soup, and it occurred to me that if the smoothie, that blender brethren, is accepted as a grab-and-go food, why not soup? I started packing cold soups with me, and I'd sip on them just as I do my morning smoothie. In this way, I opened my mind to soup beyond the bowl, and found them to be a total delight when served out of small glasses—and prepared like these spoon salads, with intensified flavor, to make a smaller serving pack a punch. You'll find blended soups like the Squash + Cider Soup, and my Pure Green Soup, which has an intoxicating back note of fennel, as well as a rich, deeply layered vegetable broth that'll nourish all winter long. All combined, these soups and salads offer exciting ways to transform your vegetable haul.

Beyond Snacks for Dinner

You can easily flesh out the spoon salads in this chapter and turn them into larger, main-dish-sized meals by spooning them on top of tender salad greens or bulking them up with rice or grains. And the blended soups can be extended and lightened up (flavor-wise) with additional broth or water. Those soups also welcome the addition of Marinated Beans with Sun-Dried Tomatoes (page 71), Lentil Snacking Granola (page 36), or pan-fried cubes of tofu (or the Chewy-Crispy Tofu Sticks with Chili-Ginger Jam Dipping Sauce on page 128, served on the side) if you'd like to make them heartier. And the Rich Vegetable Sipping Broth makes an excellent stock for cooking as well.

Small but Mighty | Salads + Soups

ROASTED RADISH + GRAPEFRUIT SALAD

This is a juicy winter salad that captures the feeling of summer with its winning combination of both succulent and fresh, snappy textures. It's also a play on bitterness. Radishes are mellowed by roasting and find bright, bittersweet partners in grapefruit supremes and the heat of fresh ginger. This salad is one to show off your knife skills (see page 52)—you'll need to make thin matchsticks of the ginger, supreme the grapefruit, and shave celery and radishes thinly. I've included instructions in the recipe, but be patient and practice your pinch grip. This can be prepared ahead, but juices will collect in the bowl as the salad sits. It'll still taste great, and the celery will retain its crunch for quite a while; serving it on the soupier side has ceviche vibes.

Serves 4

1 bunch radishes (8 to 12 medium), trimmed	Freshly ground black pepper
1 ounce fresh ginger (about a 3-inch piece), peeled	1 heavy grapefruit
	2 long celery stalks, trimmed
3 tablespoons olive oil, divided	1 tablespoon sherry vinegar
Kosher salt	¼ teaspoon sugar
	Handful torn mint leaves, for garnish

Preheat the oven to 400°F.

Set two of the radishes aside, then chop the remaining into quarters if they're medium-sized, eighths if large, and in half if small—they should all be similarly sized.

Using a sharp, sturdy knife, julienne the ginger by first cutting it into thin slabs, then stacking the slabs on top of one another, and then slicing them into matchsticks.

In a medium oven-safe skillet (such as a cast-iron one) toss the cut radishes with 2 tablespoons olive oil, the ginger, two big pinches of salt, and a few grinds of black pepper, and arrange them in the skillet cut side down. Roast for 10 minutes, stir, and then about 5 minutes more, until slightly shriveled but not completely soft.

Meanwhile, cut the grapefruit flesh into supremes: First trim off the ends of the fruit, exposing the flesh inside, so that it can stand upright on a cutting board. Using a sharp chef's knife, cut off all the peel and pith, until only a globe of fruit flesh is left. Hold this over a bowl and carefully cut into the core of the fruit between the membranes until you dislodge the flesh, and let it drop into the bowl. Squeeze the spent membranes into the bowl to extract all the juice. (It may help to look up an online video tutorial.) Separate the grapefruit segments from the juice and tear them into bite-sized pieces, placing them in a mixing bowl.

Slice the celery and reserved radishes into thin shavings and add to the bowl with the grapefruit, along with the roasted radishes, ginger, and any pooled oil from the pan.

To make the dressing, combine 1 tablespoon of the reserved grapefruit juice (gulp the rest, or reserve it for another use), the vinegar, ¼ teaspoon salt, sugar, and remaining 1 tablespoon olive oil in a small jar or bowl and shake or whisk to emulsify. Just before serving, pour over the salad and stir gently to combine. Garnish with the mint and serve. Chilled leftovers are excellent the next day, though be aware that liquid will pool in the container as it sits.

RICH VEGETABLE SIPPING BROTH

As soon as it gets cold, there's nothing I'm happier to have on hand than a broth like this one. It's rich, and strongly flavored, designed to fortify. Typically when I make stock, it's a free-for-all receptacle for vegetable scraps. But here, I've deliberately pared back the vegetable quotient to dial in the flavor. The softer leek and fennel over onions and celery are important, and there's just the right amount of sweetness from squash. It also boasts a healthful dose of sea vegetables (kombu, wakame), dried mushrooms, and ginger. Served in a mug, it brings a wonderful focus to a snacks-for-dinner meal. And I must be the last person on earth to awaken to the utility of the Instant Pot, but what a dream it is for making stock and broth. It, or any slow cooker, makes a beautiful broth, and I've included instructions below. I like to start the broth before going to bed, and then it's ready in the morning—a treat as good as a cup of coffee.

Makes 2 to 2½ quarts

1 medium leek or 3 small ones, coarsely chopped, or about 10 ounces trimmings

½ small-to-medium butternut squash (seeds, peels, and all), cubed, or about 8 ounces squash trimmings

1 medium fennel bulb plus ends and fronds, coarsely chopped, or about 12 ounces fennel trimmings

1 cup dried shiitake mushrooms, or 1 ounce mixed dried mushrooms

2 wide strips kombu

¼ cup wakame

1 ounce fresh ginger (about a 3-inch piece) cut into chunks

5 black peppercorns

1 teaspoon fennel seeds

Kosher salt, to taste

Fresh lemon juice or apple cider vinegar, for serving

Freshly ground black pepper, for serving

To make in a slow cooker: Combine all ingredients up until the salt in the bowl that fits your slow cooker device, then add enough water just to cover the solids—usually between 8 and 10 cups. Cook, set on low if you have the option, for 6 to 8 hours.

To make in a pressure cooker: Combine all ingredients up until the salt in a pressure cooker or the bowl that fits your combo cooker, then add enough water just to cover the solids—usually between 8 and 10 cups. Cook, set on high pressure, for 25 minutes, then allow for natural release.

To make on the stovetop: Combine all ingredients except for salt in a stockpot or other large pot, then add enough water just to cover the solids—usually between 8 and 10 cups. Bring to a boil, then reduce the heat to a very gentle simmer and cook, partially covered, for 2 hours, until strongly flavored and reduced slightly.

Strain the solids by pouring the contents of the pot through a sieve or a cheesecloth-lined colander set over a bowl or large pitcher. Be sure to press on the solids with a spatula to extract as much liquid as possible (the mushrooms in particular will have soaked up quite a bit). If using cheesecloth, and if cooled until safe to handle, gather up the solids in the cheesecloth and wring the liquid out.

To serve, reheat as much broth as you plan to sip in a clean saucepan or pot until it's steaming, and season with a few pinches of salt to taste (I think this is best when quite salty). Divide between mugs or cups, garnish with a twist of freshly ground black pepper, and serve with a spritz of lemon juice or splash of apple cider vinegar.

Once cooled, divide among airtight containers and refrigerate for up to 3 days, or freeze for up to 3 months.

Rich Vegetable Sipping Broth (p. 158)

Crispy Broiled Maitake Mushrooms (p. 50)

LENTILS, CARROTS + DATES WITH DILL

A carrot that's ripe, sweet, and juicy will really shine in this salad—supporting the sticky caramel notes of the dates and providing contrast, both texture- and flavor-wise, to the earthiness of the lentils. The dill is a bit of a wild card, and if you're dill averse, you can substitute tender parsley leaves, or skip the herbs altogether, but I find that the synergy of the carrots and dates, plus that of the lemon (in the vinaigrette) and dill, work in a brilliant way. For salads like this, small, firm lentils, such as French du Puy or black Beluga, work best because they hold their shape so well. If flat green or brown lentils are what you've got, just make sure to be attentive as you cook them, removing them from the heat right when they're tender, because they can be easier to overcook.

Serves 4

2/3 cup small, dark green or black lentils, such as du Puy or Beluga
Kosher salt
1 clove garlic
1 tablespoon sherry vinegar
2 tablespoons fresh lemon juice
1 teaspoon honey
Big pinch dried chili flakes
3 tablespoons olive oil
Freshly ground black pepper
1 large carrot (about 8 ounces), or 2 to 4 smaller ones
5 large dates, pitted and diced
1/4 cup dill fronds

Rinse the lentils and comb through them for stones. Place in a saucepan and add enough water to cover by about an inch. Bring to a simmer, add ½ teaspoon salt, then reduce the heat to maintain a very gentle simmer and partially cover the pan. Cook until the lentils are pleasingly tender—start tasting after 15 minutes, though they may take up to 25 minutes. If the lentils rise above the water surface, simply add a bit of hot tap water to keep them submerged. Once tender, strain off any excess liquid.

Meanwhile, to prepare the vinaigrette, mince the garlic, sprinkle it with a pinch of salt, then continue mincing and flatting it out on your cutting board using the flat side of your chef's knife until you have garlic paste. Combine this with the vinegar, lemon juice, honey, chili flakes, oil, and a few grinds of black pepper in a small jar and shake until emulsified. (Alternatively, whisk together the garlic paste with the vinegar, lemon juice, honey, chili flakes, and pepper, then whisk in the oil in a steady stream.) Pour the vinaigrette over the warm lentils and allow to marinate and cool for at least 10 to 15 minutes.

Using the large-hole side of a box grater, grate your carrot, angling it on a bias in order to get long, feathery shreds. You should have about 2 cups.

Combine the carrots and dates with the lentils in a mixing bowl. Fold in the dill just before serving. Taste, adding additional salt and/or lemon as needed.

BRUSSELS SPROUTS WITH PEANUTS + YUBA

Yuba are pasta-like skins that form on the surface of soy milk. Their unassuming, lightweight appearance belies that they're a protein- and nutrient-dense ingredient that's incredibly versatile, particularly as a stand-in for noodles in salads and stir-fries. I've had increasing success finding the Hodo brand of yuba at national grocery stores, though they're always readily available at Chinese grocers, where they're usually sold dried and just need to be soaked to rehydrate for 4 to 6 hours, or overnight (you'll need to gently unfold the large sheets and then use a sharp knife to trim them down to noodles). In this hearty salad, yuba add extra body and bounce to quickly seared Brussels sprouts, which are spiked with lime juice and pickled shallot and chili. If you've made the Baked Brussels Sprouts Chips (page 45), use the cores in here—you'll have almost exactly the right amount.

Serves 4

8 ounces Brussels sprouts, or reserved Brussels sprouts cores (see headnote)	Kosher salt
1 medium shallot, sliced into thin strips	2 tablespoons coconut oil
1 small chili (red fresno, jalapeño, or serrano), sliced into thin rounds	2½ ounces fresh yuba sheets
Juice of 2 limes (about ¼ cup)	1 Persian cucumber, cubed
	¼ cup roasted peanuts
	Toasted sesame oil

Trim off the browned root ends of the Brussels sprouts, then slice them in half through the stem. Laying the pieces flat on your cutting board, slice them into thin half-moons.

Combine the shallot, chili, lime juice, and a scant ¼ teaspoon salt in a small bowl.

Melt the coconut oil in a medium skillet over medium-high heat, then add the sprouts and a big pinch of salt. Cook them until they begin to caramelize but still retain a bit of crunch, shaking the pan every now and then, 7 to 10 minutes. Add the shallot-chili mixture to the pan and scrape up any browned bits, then remove from the heat and allow to cool slightly.

Unfold the yuba sheets, then cut them into moderately short "noodles" about 5 to 6 inches long by ⅛ inch wide by gently rolling or folding the sheet over once or twice and using a sharp chef's knife. These should be about the width of fettuccine noodles.

In a serving bowl, combine the Brussels sprouts with the yuba noodles, cucumber, and peanuts. Drizzle very lightly with the sesame oil. Taste and adjust salt and lime as needed, then serve warm or at room temperature.

SQUASH + CIDER SOUP

This soup has a striking purity of flavor—squash and cider, perfectly in balance. More than any of the other soups in this chapter, it's an intense sipper, and it's best ladled into small cups alongside other fall and winter offerings—think earthy beans, Brussels sprouts, or wintery greens. Cooking the squash on the stovetop, rather than roasting it, both speeds up and simplifies the process, and keeps it from becoming too sweet and cloying. And if breaking down a hardy winter squash is something that intimidates you, purchasing pre-peeled and -diced squash works great in this recipe. As with all pureed soups, I recommend erring on the side of caution when adding the stock. It's hard to rescue a soup that's too thin after you blend it, but one that's too thick can easily be fixed by blitzing in a bit more stock or water.

Makes about 2 quarts

2 tablespoons butter or olive oil
1 large onion, diced
3 cloves garlic, sliced
2 bay leaves
A small handful thyme sprigs
1½ teaspoons kosher salt
1 medium butternut squash (1½ to 2 pounds), peeled, seeded, and cubed

2 tablespoons apple cider vinegar
2 tablespoons whiskey or bourbon, optioinal
½ cup apple cider
About 2½ cups light-flavored stock or water
Freshly ground black pepper

In a soup pot or Dutch oven, melt the butter or warm the oil over medium heat, then add the onion, garlic, bay leaves, thyme sprigs, and salt. Cook, stirring periodically, until softened and even beginning to brown—6 to 8 minutes. Add the squash and stir to incorporate with the onions. Cook, uncovered, until it begins sticking to the pot and taking on a bit of caramelization, about 10 minutes. Raise the heat slightly and deglaze with the vinegar and whiskey, if using, scraping up the browned bits, and then add the cider. Allow the cider to bubble away for 5 to 10 minutes, until it's reduced by half. Pour in the stock—you'll need just enough to cover the vegetables so that they're easy to stir in the liquid. Once it comes to a boil, reduce the heat to establish a gentle simmer, then partially cover the pot with a lid and cook gently until the squash is soft enough that you can easily smash it against the side of the pot using a wooden spoon.

Fish out the bay leaves and thyme sprigs, then puree the soup using a handheld immersion blender or in batches in a blender or food processor, until completely smooth, using caution since the contents are hot. Return the soup to the pot and season with black pepper and additional salt if needed. Serve hot.

Brussels Sprouts with Peanuts + Yuba (p. 162)

Celery Salad with Maple-Candied Almond + Shallot (p. 169)

Squash + Cider Soup (p. 163)

CHARRED RADICCHIO WITH FARRO + BURRATA

A ball of burrata is one of my favorite secret weapons when I cook for my family in Lake Tahoe. In the summer, I go with the tried-and-true treatment of breaking the wobbly balls over platters of ripe supper tomatoes and stone fruit. But in the winter, when chicories are one of the more exciting vegetable offerings available, this is our celebration salad. It combines creaminess and bitterness with a just-sweet-enough vinaigrette. I prefer white balsamic vinegar here—it's generally a little less sweet, and has a gentler flavor. The farro and the radicchio can be cooked up to a few hours in advance, but the salad should only be assembled right before you eat.

Serves 4

Kosher salt
1 cup farro, rinsed
2 medium heads radicchio
2 tablespoons plus 2 teaspoons white balsamic vinegar, divided
3 tablespoons olive oil, plus additional for drizzling

1 tablespoon white wine vinegar
2 teaspoons Dijon mustard
2 teaspoons maple syrup
Freshly ground black pepper
2 small spheres (8 ounces total) burrata
Freshly ground black pepper

Bring a saucepan of water to boil and salt generously, then add the farro. Cook until the grains are just tender—start tasting after about 15 minutes, or use the package instructions as a guide. Drain and transfer to a mixing bowl, spreading them in a thin layer to help them cool.

Meanwhile, peel off any discolored or limp outer leaves of the radicchio, then cut in half lengthwise through the stem. Set cut side up, sprinkle them with the 2 teaspoons white balsamic vinegar and a few pinches of salt, and let sit for about 15 minutes.

To grill the radicchio, heat your grill (or a portion of it) to high. Brush the radicchio lightly with olive oil. When the grill is hot, cook them cut side down for 2 to 3 minutes directly over the flame until charred and browned. Flip and char the other side until it takes on some color as well. (Alternatively, to broil the radicchio, preheat your broiler and set it to high. Arrange the radicchio cut side up on a baking sheet and brush lightly with olive oil. Cook directly under the heat source until charred and browned, about 2 to 3 minutes, then flip and repeat for the outer sides.) Transfer to a cutting board or plate, and when safe to handle, chop coarsely.

To prepare the vinaigrette, combine the remaining 2 tablespoons white balsamic, white wine vinegar, mustard, maple syrup, ¼ teaspoon salt, and 3 tablespoons olive oil in a jar and shake until emulsified. (Alternatively, whisk together the vinegars, mustard, maple syrup, and salt in a small bowl, then whisk in the oil in a steady stream.)

Stir about half of the dressing into the farro, then scatter the radicchio on top. Break the burrata on top and drizzle with remaining dressing. Finish with freshly ground black pepper and a few pinches of salt.

Gently Fried Nuts with Rosemary (p. 51)

Orange + Mustard Marinated Asparagus (p. 67)

Charred Radicchio with Farro + Burrata (p. 166)

PURE GREEN SOUP

This is a simple soup through and through—a short list of ingredients, a straightforward preparation, a modest appearance—but it's one of those dishes that really adds up to much more. It has heartiness and is flavorful in a more forward way than I typically find with greens-based soups, in large part because there's no "flab" or starchy filler. Just a pure greenness. Part of what helps achieve this is zucchini, providing the body and thickening properties that might more typically come from potato or a dairy thickener, and I love how it deepens rather than muffles the "green" flavors. Fennel, too, sautéed and then pureed along with the rest of the ingredients, contributes to the body while also layering on flavor. The result is a simple soup that still packs a punch, perfect to be enjoyed in small doses alongside a few other snacky items. And a nice, peppery olive oil goes a long way as a finishing drizzle.

Makes about 2 quarts

3 tablespoons olive oil, plus additional for drizzling

10 ounces spinach, tough stems trimmed if mature

1 small or ½ large bulb fennel, cored and diced

2 celery stalks, diced

1 medium onion, diced

1 medium zucchini (6 ounces), diced

3 garlic cloves, sliced

½ teaspoon kosher salt, plus additional to taste

4 cups vegetable stock

In a soup pot, warm 1 tablespoon of the olive oil over medium heat. Add the spinach and cook, stirring, until wilted. Transfer to a plate.

Return the pot to the heat and warm the remaining 2 tablespoons oil, then add the fennel, celery, onion, zucchini, garlic, and ½ teaspoon salt. Stir to evenly coat in the oil, then allow to sweat until the onions and fennel are softened and translucent, but not browned, 12 to 15 minutes. Taste a piece to test. Cover with the stock, bring to a simmer, then cook for 10 minutes more to allow flavors to meld.

Transfer the contents of the pot and the spinach to a blender and puree until very smooth. (You can also use an immersion blender, but you'll need to be very thorough.) Wipe out the pot, then return the soup to it and reheat. Taste for salt. Serve hot, drizzled with your best olive oil.

CELERY SALAD WITH MAPLE-CANDIED ALMOND + SHALLOT

Celery's status as a zero-calorie diet food has overshadowed its satisfying, saline crunch, and I think it's an incredibly underappreciated vegetable. Hopefully, this salad helps to set the record straight. The celery provides the body, creating a quenching base that's full of texture, and further personality comes in the form of little tangles of maple-candied shallots and almonds, ripe pear, and chunks of Parmesan. It keeps well for a few hours packed in an airtight container in the fridge, but the celery will gradually lose its crunch and release its water once it is dressed. Do take care to slice the shallot evenly and thinly, else they won't become properly crisp or mingle with the maple and almonds—a mandoline is ideal.

Serves 4 to 6

2 medium shallots

6 tablespoons olive oil, divided

$1/3$ cup raw almonds, chopped in half

1 tablespoon plus 2 teaspoons maple syrup

$1/4$ teaspoon plus a pinch kosher salt

1 tablespoon balsamic vinegar

1 tablespoon white wine vinegar

2 teaspoons Dijon mustard

4 long, crisp celery stalks, plus the celery heart

1 pear or apple

3 tablespoons coarsely cubed Parmesan cheese

Freshly ground black pepper

Trim off the root and tip ends of the shallots, then halve them lengthwise and peel off the skin. Using a mandoline or working carefully with a sharp chef's knife, slice them into thin strips—not quite paper-thin, but slightly less than ⅛ inch.

In a medium skillet, warm 3 tablespoons of the oil over medium heat, then add the shallots and cook until softened and translucent, 5 to 7 minutes. Stir in the almonds and continue cooking until they're lightly browned and fragrant and the shallots have become a bit crispy and frizzled, another 10 to 15 minutes. Raise the heat slightly and add 1 tablespoon of the maple syrup and a big pinch of salt. Cook for another minute, allowing the syrup to thicken and clusters of shallot and almond to form, then remove it from the heat. Transfer the solids to a plate to cool.

To make the vinaigrette, combine the vinegars, mustard, remaining 2 teaspoons maple syrup, ¼ teaspoon salt, and remaining 3 tablespoons olive oil in a small jar, and shake to emulsify. (Alternatively, whisk the vinegars, mustard, maple syrup, and salt together in a bowl, then whisk in the olive oil while adding it in a steady stream.)

Slice the celery stalks on a bias into ¼-inch-thick pieces and place them in a serving bowl. Mince the celery heart finely and add to the bowl as well. Core the pear or apple and cut it into pieces about the same size as the celery stalks—¼-inch-thick pieces—and add to the bowl, along with the Parmesan. Gently break up the shallot-almond topping into small pieces and scatter on top of the vegetables, then toss with the dressing. Top with several grinds of black pepper. Serve within a few hours.

FRESH ASPARAGUS WITH WHITE BEANS + CRISPY CHEDDAR

When asparagus is freshly picked and in season, it has incredible vibrancy—sweet and green-tasting, with some slight nuttiness and a terrific, juicy texture and I'm happy eating it in its raw state, shaved down into thin pieces that break up its fibrousness. There are lots of spring salads made from asparagus ribbons, using a vegetable peeler to create them, but I find that to be a difficult and tedious process. I have better luck using my sharp chef's knife and taking my time to slice the asparagus into thin coins on a steep bias, which also makes them more spoon-friendly. In this recipe, if you've got good, fresh asparagus, keep it raw, but if not, you can very quickly sauté the prepped asparagus coins. For a little salty crispiness that mimics croutons or crispy bread crumbs, a cheddar frico that is crumbled over the salad just before serving.

Serves 4

1 cup coarsely grated sharp cheddar
   cheese
Freshly ground black pepper
½ pound thick asparagus stalks
   (about 6)
1 lemon
½ teaspoon honey

½ teaspoon kosher salt
3 tablespoons good olive oil
One 14.5-ounce can white beans
   (cannellini, great northern, navy),
   drained and rinsed
2 handfuls watercress sprigs or baby
   arugula

Place a medium nonstick skillet over medium heat, then sprinkle the cheese all over the surface in an even layer. Sprinkle with a few grinds of black pepper. Allow the cheese to melt and then bubble as the oils separate from the solids and the cheese darkens slightly to a pale brown color and begins to turn crisp, 4 to 6 minutes. Use a thin spatula to gently loosen it from the pan and transfer it onto a plate, where it will further crispen up as it cools.

Snap the woody ends off the asparagus. Then, working one piece at a time, slice it into thin coins on a steep bias. Taste—if the asparagus is farmers' market fresh, it should have a juicy texture and taste great on its own. But if you don't like the taste of it raw, heat a splash of olive oil in the nonstick pan and briefly sauté the asparagus until just tender, 1 to 2 minutes.

To make the dressing, zest the lemon and then juice it into a small bowl. Add the honey and salt, then whisk in the olive oil.

In a mixing bowl, combine the asparagus with the beans and watercress sprigs. Toss with the dressing to taste. Just before serving, crumble the cheddar frico over the salad.

Fresh Asparagus with
White Beans + Crispy Cheddar
(p. 170)

Gingery Cucumber–Almond Soup (p. 172)

Focaccia Crackers (p. 187)

GINGERY CUCUMBER-ALMOND SOUP

I've made a lot of different cold cucumber soups over the years (cucumber being one of my favorite vegetables), often using a base of milk and yogurt. But this dairy-free version has a punchiness and creaminess that the others do not, and with the gentle heat of the ginger against the cooling cucumber, it's incredibly quenching. If cucumbers are in season, use them, but I often use the long English cucumbers (sold shrink-wrapped in plastic), too. Whatever cucumber you choose, use your judgment as to whether it should be peeled—if the skin is thin and tender, it's not necessary, but tough, waxy skin can get in the way of the soup. If you've ever encountered what I call a POS avocado (these, of course, are the ones that feel great from the outside but are splotched with brown threads and bruises when you cut them open), you can just blend it up in this soup and no one will ever know any better. Last, because of the avocado, it can oxidize and turn brown over time, so it's best to enjoy it within a day of making it.

Makes 1 quart, 4 to 6 servings

¼ cup almonds, covered with water and soaked for 1 to 4 hours

1 ounce fresh ginger (about a 3-inch piece), peeled and coarsely chopped

2 English or hothouse cucumbers (1½ pounds), peeled if desired, divided

½ ripe avocado

2 tablespoons olive oil

1 tablespoon fresh lemon juice

1 tablespoon plus 1 teaspoon white wine vinegar

¾ teaspoon kosher salt

Freshly ground black or white pepper

½ teaspoon dried oregano

¼ teaspoon ground cumin

Drain and rinse the almonds, then place in a high-speed blender pitcher along with ½ cup water and the ginger. Liquefy the mixture. Then add one and a half of the cucumbers (reserving remaining for the garnish), the avocado, olive oil, lemon juice, 1 tablespoon vinegar, and salt. Puree thoroughly, until very smooth, then taste, seasoning with pepper and more salt or vinegar as needed. Transfer the soup to a container, and if you have time, chill in the fridge for at least 2 hours.

(If you don't have a high-speed blender, blend the almonds and ginger with ½ cup water until as liquefied as possible, then pour the mixture through a cheesecloth-lined colander or nutmilk bag to remove the fibrous pieces—standard blenders just can't break these down as well. Return the strained liquid to the blender and add the remaining ingredients in step 1.)

Dice the remaining cucumber and combine with the oregano, cumin, and remaining 1 teaspoon vinegar in a small bowl. Taste the soup once more, adjusting the flavors if needed, then serve in small cups, garnished with the seasoned cucumbers and drizzled with a few drops of olive oil.

PEAK-SEASON GAZPACHO WITH WATERMELON

There are a lot of things that a year-round greenhouse tomato is good for, but gazpacho isn't one of them. In gazpacho, you want your tomatoes *heavy*—those bruised, blemished, leaky ones sold at a discount are actually ideal, because that ripe, savory juice is what makes gazpacho a soup rather than a tomato salad. And ever since I first tried a version of gazpacho that included watermelon, I've never looked back. The watermelon cuts the acid and doubles the quench factor. Grating the tomatoes produces pulp, maintaining the juiciness of the tomato flesh, and if your watermelon is equally ripe, it will also fall apart to create a beautifully textured soup base.

Serves 4

3 cups cubed, seeded (or seedless), peeled ripe watermelon (about 2 pounds)	1 red or green jalapeno, cored and seeded
	½ medium red onion
2 heavy, ripe tomatoes (1½ to 2 pounds), quartered and cored	3 to 4 tablespoons red wine vinegar
	2 tablespoons olive oil
1 medium cucumber, peeled	¾ teaspoon kosher salt
1 sweet bell pepper, cored and seeded	Freshly ground black pepper

Using a food processor fitted with the grater attachment (large holes), grate the watermelon and tomatoes. You'll need to do this in batches—watch to make sure that the liquid doesn't overflow. Most of the tomato skins will be left in the feeding tube, and you can snack on them or reserve them for another use. Transfer to a large mixing bowl. (To make this without a food processor, simply place a box grater in a wide bowl and grate the tomatoes and watermelon into it by hand.)

Cut the cucumber, peppers, and red onion by first slicing them into thin strips or matchsticks, and then rotating the strips 90 degrees to chop into a fine dice. (Alternatively, switch to the chopping blade of your food processor and pulse until these ingredients are finely chopped.)

Add the vegetables to the mixing bowl along with 3 tablespoons of the red wine vinegar, the olive oil, the salt, and several grinds of black pepper, and mix to combine. Taste, adding additional vinegar or salt as needed. Cover and chill for at least an hour. Serve cold, drizzled with additional olive oil.

Hibiscus + Grapefruit, Hot or Cold (p. 203)

Summer Tomato Salad with Frizzled Shallots (p. 175)

Australian Zucchini Slice (p. 119)

SUMMER TOMATO SALAD WITH FRIZZLED SHALLOTS

Soy sauce and tomatoes are such a wonderful combination, something well known across many Asian cuisines, of course, but perhaps not so much here in the United States. So once you've tired of eating the peak summer fruit sprinkled with just salt and pepper, give this salad a try. Ripe, seasonal tomatoes will make a world of difference, and my favorite ones are those sold in pint and quarter baskets at the farmers' market in a mix of various colors, shapes, and sizes, which can all be cut down into irregular shapes to create a dazzling platter. Frizzled shallots add texture and some salty richness, and their cooking oil forms the base of the soy-sauce-spiked dressing. Raid your herb garden for the garnish—I love the combination of purple basil and cilantro here, but there's flexibility, and I encourage you to work with what you've got.

Serves 4

3 medium shallots
Neutral-tasting oil, such as grapeseed
    or avocado oil
2 tablespoons dark soy sauce
2 teaspoons rice vinegar
¼ teaspoon kosher salt

¼ teaspoon ground black pepper
1½ pounds (about 2 pints) small and
    medium-sized, ripe tomatoes, ideally
    of various colors and shapes
Generous handful of tender, fresh herbs:
    basil (any variety), cilantro, chives

Trim off the tips of the shallots and peel them, keeping them whole. Use a mandoline to shave them into paper-thin rings, using the root ends as something of a handle. You can do this with a knife if you're confident, but they need to be uniformly thick in order to fry evenly.

In a saucepan or skillet, heat about ¼ inch of the oil over medium heat. To test the temperature, dip in a shallot ring—it should sizzle on contact. If it doesn't, wait another minute or two. Once hot, add the shallots and cook, stirring often, until they release their water, and become reddish brown and crispy. This will happen quickly toward the end, so don't walk away from the pan. Use a slotted spoon to transfer the frizzled shallots to a paper towel-lined plate. Once the oil has cooled, strain it into a tall measuring glass.

To make the dressing, measure 2 tablespoons of the shallot oil in a small bowl, and whisk in the soy sauce, rice vinegar, salt, and pepper.

Just before serving, cut the tomatoes into bite-sized pieces. I love irregular shapes here, which you can do by slicing on the bias, or chopping into thirds, or incorporating a combination of rounds and wedges. Arrange the tomatoes over a serving platter and drizzle the dressing over them to taste. Tear and sprinkle the herbs on top, followed by the frizzled shallots, and serve.

Everyday Flowers with Blake

My friend Blake Adair Bachman is one of the most generous people I know and a terrifically inventive cook—which is enough to qualify him as an ideal dinner host—but because of his background in studio art, interior design, and floral design, he also knows how to make every single moment of a meal extra sensory. Whether it's a coursed meal for a group of eight, a last-minute hangout where dinner's been delivered, or a snacks-for-dinner spread, he tweaks the lighting, sets out nice glassware, incorporates some gorgeous fabric in the form of a napkin or tablecloth, and there are always flowers. Inspired by him, I've begun incorporating flowers into my life more regularly, and the benefits are vast: they add color, fragrance, and a sense of intention to a room, and they enliven even the most routine of Tuesday-night dinners. Blake was generous enough to share a few of his pro tips. If you aren't a flower person, trust me that it's never too late.

FIND FLOWERS CLOSE TO HOME: If you have flower beds of your own, start there, with roses, lilacs, irises, or whatever is in your yard. If you have the space—a yard, patio, or some space on a fire escape—consider planting flowers that can be brought inside when you're entertaining. "Not just smaller pots to use as centerpieces," Blake says, "but even something larger like a showy geranium or hybrid ever-blooming sunflower." Those can also be cut from to build arrangements. Similarly, find local and in-season flowers at your farmers' market. Flowers from the grocery store can be used to supplement if needed.

FOCUS ON WHAT'S IN SEASON: As with produce, lead with what's seasonally abundant. "Start with several bunches of the same type of flower, and steer clear of mixed bouquets," Blake says, meaning that one big bunch of peonies will be more striking than a few different things scattered about or combined in one vase. Flowering herbs like oregano and basil and edible flowers like nasturtiums add texture and fragrance to the table, too. Peak-season fruits and vegetables can also stand in as a colorful table decoration, like a bowl of citrus, pears, or vegetables, like squash and eggplant. Opt for small or unusual sizes and shapes—honeynut squash, clementines or tangerines, small crab- or Pink Lady apples, for example—and leave the stems attached to boost the visual interest.

USE YOUR OWN GLASSWARE TO DISPLAY THEM: There's no need to build a big collection of vases, because everyday water and juice glasses, and repurposed containers like jars and even medium-sized coffee tins, are perfect for creating your own arrangements. Glasses that flare slightly, aren't too tall, and have a narrow base are the most versatile, though ones that are too small might be prone to tipping over at the table. The thinking here is that shorter glasses, cups, and vases keep the arrangement below eye level.

For table arrangements, Blake thinks of vases in three sizes, and as they get bigger, you can increase the stem length (as well as the number of flowers):

· **Small:** This is the size of a juice glass, or a can of tomato paste. Use it for a few smaller garden roses, flowering herbs or lavender, or a small handful of tulips cut short enough that they shoot upward.

· **Medium:** This is about the size of a water glass or a soup or soda can, and it's great for larger roses with some of their leaves still attached, or irises, daffodils, anemones, and ranunculus.

· **Large:** This is a wide-but-not-too-tall container or vase, roughly the size of a 28-ounce can of tomatoes, and perfect for three to five stems of hydrangea ("one of the easiest flowers to arrange"), as well as lilies, flowering foliage, and geranium.

OPT FOR ORGANIC ARRANGEMENTS: First things first, always cut flowers with caution. It's like salting food: you can always trim more, but once you've made a cut, you can't trim less. And then as you add flowers to a vase, begin by aiming to create an organic-feeling arrangement. "Try and go a little wild with the composition," Blake says, because organic movement always feels natural and looks arresting. And for "filler," use smaller baby ("spray") roses, geranium leaves, or mint or other leafy herbs.

CONSIDER WITH FOOD: Extra-fragrant flowers like lilies or hyacinth should be positioned a safe distance from the table so as to not interfere with food. At the table, Blake prefers shorter arrangements because they stay below eye level—his rule of thumb is "flowers low, candles high." If you've got tall arrangements, place them at one end of the table rather than in the center. Last, the flowers and other table decorations can always be sorted out ahead of time. You can buy flowers up to a few days in advance, and unless the heat and humidity is strong, they should stay vibrant—particularly if kept in a cool place.

THE FOOD IS A DECORATION, TOO: "Butter, olive oil, little bowls and glass jars of condiments, water in glass bottles or carafes, and wine all mix with the more literal and sometimes functional table decorations," he says. To that end, the shapes and contrasts of your crudités, rustic crackers, bread, and spiced nuts and snack mixes can certainly be thought of as decoration, particularly those items that can be set out on the table early on, before it's time to sit down to eat.

AND A QUICK LIGHTING TIP: When Blake adjusts the lighting around a dining table, he's always thinking about how he can uplift and amplify the texture and warmth of candlelight. If there are candles at the table, this means avoiding cool lighting altogether, such as that created by fluorescent or many LED lights that give off a bright white or bluish hue (check the labels on your lightbulbs to know for sure). Then create patches of gentle warmth around the surrounding tables and corners of the room with lamps, and utilize a dimmer switch on any overhead lighting that might be needed. "The warmer the better," he says. The reason why candles and low, warm light are both so common at restaurants is because the light feels flattering and comforting. If this is something you hadn't thought about before, you're about to start noticing it everywhere—the spaces that invite us to linger are almost always gently, warmly lit, and why should your dinner table be any different?

STURDY SUPPORT | CRACKERS, BREADS, CHIPS

I know you might be tempted to skip past this chapter—after all, there's a whole aisle at the grocery store devoted to crackers, fresh bread at your favorite bakery, and endless varieties of chips available at every convenience store. But I think you'll find these recipes to be incredibly rewarding, and you'll be surprised by how doable they are. Homemade crackers? Yes! In about an hour, most of which is passive waiting or baking time.

Because I'm always writing recipes and always cooking, my friends and family have come to expect things like homemade crackers and focaccia from me. But as I've shared my recipes for these snacks over the years, I've heard a common refrain: "Nobody believed I made these!" We live in a world where few people expect anyone to go to the trouble of making from scratch what can be easily procured elsewhere. Most people assume "wheat crackers" must come from a box, so when I tell you that it's actually not that difficult to make them on your own, I hope you'll seize the opportunity to impress. (And to that end, these vessels all make terrific gifts, wrapped up in kraft paper or a tin, for a dinner party host or a holiday exchange.)

I think of these recipes as "vessels," because they serve a logistical purpose: they scoop up dip, forklift toppings, soak up the dregs of a flavorful marinade, and then safely navigate them to your mouth. Textures vary, from tender-crisp crackers to snappy pita chips to a plush, wheaty focaccia. Sometimes they also function as a palate cleanser, resetting your taste buds between bites of rich or strongly flavored dishes. And while you wouldn't intentionally make them the focus of a meal, these homemade treats are so special and unexpected, sometimes they can't help but claim the spotlight.

Beyond Snacks for Dinner

All the crackers in this chapter are make-ahead friendly, and if packed safely, they're sturdy enough to survive mail shipments and other forms of transport. In this way, aside from them being terrific for all types of snacking needs, they make great gifts for holidays and other types of food baskets. Additionally, the focaccia bread in this chapter makes the best slab sandwiches imaginable.

MY IDEAL FOCACCIA

My ideal version of focaccia goes beyond soft and fluffy; for me, the most important quality is a well-structured plushness, so that a thin slice has enough muscle to stand upright, aided by a deeply bronzed, crisp crust on both the top and the bottom. In addition to the sunny flavor of olive oil, I also like some wheaty, tangy flavor in the bread. And I prefer it a little thinner, rather than tall. It took years of fussing and tweaking, but I've finally achieved my ideal focaccia, and I'm very proud to share it with you here.

There are a couple important steps. First is what's called a preferment ("poolish" in French bread making, and "biga" in Italian, or sometimes called a sponge), where a small amount of flour, water, and yeast are left to bubble away, creating something of a hack sourdough starter. The second is the bulk rise, which takes 24 to 48 hours in the fridge, interrupted with a few "stretches" of the dough. These steps contribute significantly to the structure and flavor of the finished bread, and the preferment even helps to extend its quickly diminishing freshness. As with all bread making, much of the labor here is in exercising patience and planning ahead. Because fresh focaccia is so fleeting, try to eat it on the day it's baked.

Serves 6

100 grams (¾ cup plus 1 tablespoon) stone-ground spelt, whole-wheat, or rye flour	355 grams (3½ cups plus 2 tablespoons) all-purpose flour
370 grams (1⅔ cups) plus 1½ tablespoons water, divided	8 grams (1 tablespoon) plus ½ teaspoon kosher salt
½ teaspoon instant dry yeast (preferably Saf-Instant—see page 26)	3½ tablespoons olive oil, divided
5 grams (1 teaspoon) honey or granulated sugar	Butter or nonstick cooking spray, for greasing
	Coarse kosher salt or flaky finishing salt, for sprinkling on top

Stir together the spelt or whole-wheat flour, 125 grams (½ cup) water, and the yeast in a medium mixing bowl until smooth. Cover (a silicone lid works great for this) and let stand at room temperature until the mixture has loosened up and its surface is dappled with air bubbles, 3 to 4 hours.

Add 245 grams (1 cup plus 1 tablespoon) water and the honey to the bowl and stir with a spatula to incorporate. Then stir in the all-purpose flour and 8 grams salt until a mass forms. Transfer to a 2-quart container that has an airtight lid, or use the same mixing bowl and coat all over with 2 tablespoons of the olive oil. Cover with an airtight lid or seal tightly with plastic wrap and place it in the refrigerator for 24 to 48 hours.

(cont.)

Two or three times a day, try to remember to "stretch" the dough by pulling it up at four points around the perimeter of the dough and folding the flaps back over the center, then flipping the mass over so that you've got a tidy ball; you'll be able to gauge the structure of the dough developing as you do this. It should roughly double in size, though it'll deflate slightly each time you stretch it. After this bulk rise, the dough should be aerated all over with tiny bubbles—it'll feel a bit buoyant and will jiggle a bit if you give the container a gentle shake.

Three to four hours before you want to bake, remove the dough from the refrigerator and leave to warm up in its container for an hour. Grease a baking sheet with butter or nonstick cooking spray (olive oil unfortunately doesn't work here—the baked bread will glue itself to the pan; thank you to Alexandra Stafford for broadcasting this tip), and gently scrape the dough onto the pan, stretching it out slightly to shape it into an approximate rectangle centered in the pan but not stretched to the edges. Try not to handle the dough too much at this point. Lightly rub a small amount of olive oil over its surface and cover with a piece of plastic wrap, then proof for another 2 to 3 hours, until puffed up to roughly double in size. The surface will look tauter, but it'll be extra buoyant and jiggly.

Preheat the oven to 425°F, placing racks in the top and bottom thirds of the oven. If you have a baking steel or stone, place it on the lower rack, allowing 30 minutes for it to heat up.

Once the oven is hot, whisk together remaining 1½ tablespoons olive oil and 1½ tablespoons water in a small bowl or liquid measuring cup until emulsified. Dimple the dough by pressing all over the surface with your three middle fingers, pushing all the way down until you feel the baking sheet, which will help to level it off slightly into an even thickness. Don't stretch it to the edges, but by this point, after its second rise and the dimpling, it should fill most of the pan. Drizzle the oil-and-water mixture all over, letting it pool in the divots, and sprinkle evenly with ½ teaspoon finishing salt.

Bake for 20 minutes in the lower third of the oven, then move to the top rack of the oven for about 10 minutes more, until well browned. If you tuck a metal spatula underneath the bread, the base should be evenly golden-brown and crisp all over—if it's not, bake for another 5 minutes or so.

Transfer the bread from the baking sheet to a cooling rack and cool for at least 15 minutes before slicing. This is best eaten on the day it's baked, but once cooled, you can freeze individual portions and rewarm them by wrapping them in foil and placing in a preheated 350°F oven or toaster oven for about 15 minutes. Leftovers also make excellent crackers (see page 187).

My Focaccia Game Plan: Two days before I want to eat the foccacia, I'll stir together the preferment (step 1), usually right before dinner. Then before bed I mix it up with the remaining dough ingredients, scrape it into a container, and put it in the fridge (step 2). Over the next two days, when I remember, I'll "stretch" the dough a few times (step 3). Then, on the day I want to eat the bread (often in the morning or just before lunch), I pull that from the fridge, let it warm up, give it its final rise on a baking sheet, and bake it off (step 4 through the end of the recipe).

FOCACCIA CRACKERS

Sometimes it can feel like a personal failure to "waste" bread by not eating it while it's fresh. But when repurposed right, stale bread can be transformed into something just as good as the original. I used to work at a restaurant where the bread basket was made in house, and from the day-old bread we always made crackers that went right back into the bread basket. In revisiting that method with my leftover focaccia, I came to realize that there are two important rules of making crackers this way. The first is a relatively low temperature, which slowly but thoroughly cooks out the water from the bread without causing the crackers to burn. The second is a longer-than-one-might-think cooking time, which ensures that the crackers are toasted all the way through; any parts of the cracker that are still a bit bready and soft will harden when the crackers cool. I love the drama of creating long, skinny crackers from leftover focaccia, and then breaking them into smaller pieces at the table, but you can trim these down to any shape you please as long as you slice them about ¼ inch thick. And you can certainly take any liberties you like as far as seasonings go—dried herbs, hard cheese, spice blends—but I like this simple salt-and-pepper treatment best.

Yield varies

¼ to ½ recipe leftover My Ideal Focaccia (page 185)	Kosher salt
2 tablespoons olive oil	Freshly ground black pepper

Preheat the oven to 325°F.

Using a serrated knife, cut the bread into long slabs about ¼ inch thick. Trim them down to smaller crackers if you prefer.

Pour the olive oil onto a baking sheet and rub it evenly across the base. A quarter loaf of focaccia will need a full baking sheet—if you've got half a loaf leftover, prepare a second baking sheet with another 2 tablespoons oil. Arrange the bread slices in a single layer on top, as many as will fit. Press each piece into the oil so that it soaks some up and then flip it over, then season liberally with salt and pepper. The goal is to have each piece evenly and lightly oiled.

Transfer to the oven and bake for 25 to 40 minutes, until evenly golden browned and crisp all the way through. Test by breaking one in half—it should snap cleanly, and if there's any pliability, allow more time for it to toast.

Once cooled, store the crackers in an airtight container for a week or more.

CRISPY PARMESAN-PECAN STRIPS

A part of a snacky dinner or appetizers spread, these crackers are the unassuming minor character that everybody remembers the next day. They're nutty, cheesy, fragrant, and have an absolutely delectable snap. When baking them, look for an even, deep golden brown. If you're not sure that they're browned well enough, give them a few more minutes—the more deeply golden they are, the more aromatic and toasty the flavor. Also, the flaky salt sprinkled over the top is what brings out the flavor of the pecans, so make sure to sprinkle it evenly and liberally.

Makes 25 to 30 strips

¾ cup (95 grams) all-purpose flour
⅓ cup (35 grams) chopped pecans
1 cup (50 grams) finely grated, lightly
   packed Parmesan cheese
½ teaspoon ground black pepper, plus
   additional to garnish

½ teaspoon sugar
¼ teaspoon baking powder
4 tablespoons cold butter, cubed
2 to 3 tablespoons ice water
Flaky salt

Combine the flour, pecans, Parmesan, pepper, sugar, and baking powder in the bowl of a food processor and pulse until the nuts are finely ground. Add the butter, pulsing until it's broken down into pea-sized pieces. Sprinkle 2 tablespoons water over the mixture and pulse until a dough begins to form, adding another tablespoon if needed.

(To make without a food processor: First pound the pecans in a mortar and pestle or chop on a cutting board until finely ground, then combine with the cheese and other dry ingredients in a mixing bowl. Use a pastry cutter or your hands to quickly blend in the cold butter until you achieve pea-sized bits of butter, then stir in enough ice water just until the mixture comes together in large, moist crumbles.)

Dump the crumbles onto a piece of plastic wrap and, working from the outside part of the plastic, shape into a rectangle about ½ inch thick. Wrap tightly and refrigerate for at least 30 minutes and up to 2 days.

Prepare two pieces of parchment 8 inches by 11 inches, and one larger piece to function as a work surface. Cut the dough into two equally sized rectangles.

Place one piece of dough on the larger, work-surface parchment and set the smaller piece on top of the dough. Use a rolling pin to roll the dough out in smooth, gentle motions from its center, to cover as much of the top piece of parchment as possible. The rolled dough doesn't need to have perfect edges, but try as best as you can to roll it evenly. Flip the sandwiched dough over so that the larger piece is on top, and gently peel off the parchment paper. Use a sharp chef's knife or pizza cutter to score the dough into long, thin strips about ¾ inch thick, then poke it all over with the tines of a fork. Slide the crackers (parchment sheet and all) onto one end of a standard baking sheet. Repeat with the other piece of dough and slide it onto the opposite end of the same baking sheet. (Side by side, they should fit perfectly.) Sprinkle generously and evenly with flaky salt and pepper. Transfer the pan to the freezer and preheat the oven to 350°F.

Bake for 20 to 30 minutes, rotating the pan every 10 minutes, until well browned all over and crisp. If the edges start to darken too quickly, reduce the oven temperature by 15 degrees and extend the cooking time as necessary to achieve full browning. Cool, then break the baked crackers into strips and store in an airtight container for up to a week.

SALT + PEPPER WHEAT CRACKERS

These crackers have a satisfying snap, a flaky texture, and a wholesome wheat flavor permeated with olive oil. *And* they can be ready to eat in about an hour! The chia seeds lend a bit of tenderness to the cracker—think of it as a chia egg—and the cornmeal brings a delightful sandiness. My method for rolling them out may seem finicky, but this strategy makes it easier to roll out the crackers thinly, supplies an easy guide for the shape, alleviates the need to transfer the thin dough after rolling, and eliminates adding extra flour during the rolling. This recipe doubles very well if you need a larger yield; just divide the dough into two pieces before rolling it out.

Makes one 11-by-18-inch baking sheet of crackers, enough to serve 6

½ cup (65 grams) all-purpose flour

½ cup (65 grams) whole-wheat flour

1 tablespoon chia seeds, ground to a coarse powder in a spice grinder or mortar and pestle

1 tablespoon cornmeal

½ teaspoon baking powder

¼ teaspoon kosher salt

2½ tablespoons olive oil, plus extra for brushing

¼ cup cold water

Coarse or flaky salt

Coarsely ground black pepper

Preheat the oven to 375°F.

In a mixing bowl, whisk together the flours, ground chia seeds, cornmeal, baking powder, and salt until well combined. Drizzle the olive oil into the mixture and stir with a fork until the mixture forms moist crumbles. Add the water and continue stirring with a fork until the mixture begins to come together; like with pie crust, you don't want to overwork it. If you pinch a small handful and it doesn't cohere, add another teaspoon of water. Knead for about 30 seconds to bring together the dough and shape it into a rectangle. Wrap it in plastic and allow to rest in the refrigerator for about 20 minutes.

Trim a piece of parchment paper to fit inside a standard baking sheet (11 inches by 18 inches) with no overhang. Lay out a larger sheet of parchment on a work area, place the dough in its center, and set the trimmed parchment on top. Roll out the mixture until it's uniformly thin and covers as much of the top-piece of parchment as possible (it doesn't need to be perfectly shaped). Flip the whole parchment-cracker parcel over and peel off the larger piece of parchment. Brush with olive oil, then sprinkle generously with the coarse or flaky salt and black pepper. Use a sharp knife to cut the sheet into any shape you prefer (I prefer long strips), then slide the crackers onto the baking sheet, using the bottom sheet of parchment as a sled.

Bake for 20 to 30 minutes, until the crackers are browned to a chestnut color and crisp. Cool completely. Stored in an airtight container, the crackers will keep for at least a week.

THINNER, CRISPER PITA CHIPS

These will sound fussy, and maybe they are, but if you've ever shared my opinion that pita chips are often too much like a dried-out pita and not enough like a crunchy chip—well, maybe you'll appreciate the fussiness. Here you'll not only split each pita pocket in half to get two thin half-moons, but you'll also then flatten those pieces out with a rolling pin before tossing with oil and baking. What this does is guarantee thin "chips" that, once baked in the oven, become shatteringly crisp. They're seasoned only with salt here so as to make them as versatile as possible with dips and other snack spreads, but almost any dried spices or herbs can be used to add personality. This quantity fits well on one baking sheet; you can easily double or triple the recipe to bake off a larger batch, as long as you double or triple the baking sheets used.

Serves 4

3 store-bought pitas	Kosher salt
3 tablespoons olive oil or melted butter, or 2 tablespoons melted ghee	

Preheat the oven to 350°F.

Cut each pita in half to create two semicircles, then tuck a sharp knife into each "pocket" to slice the halves open, forming two thin half-moon-shaped pieces. Using a rolling pin, forcefully flatten each piece out. Cut or tear into bite-sized pieces and arrange on a baking sheet in an even, slightly overlapping single layer. Drizzle with the olive oil and use your hands to ensure each piece is coated. Sprinkle with a few pinches of salt.

Transfer to the oven and bake until golden brown and crisp, 20 to 30 minutes, stirring once. Once cooled, they'll keep for up to a week stored in an airtight container.

SESAME + DATE SLICE-AND-BAKE BISCUITS

More tender than crisp, these English biscuit–style crackers are just sweet enough to function as an accent piece to a cheese board, but also bring character to a range of other snacks—spoon salads, creamy soups, a few dips, and a platter of crudités. The method is similar to making other short pastries like shortbread or piecrust, where you'll want to do your best to not overwork the dough after the water is added. I find that I get more consistent results using a food processor, but you can also make them by hand—just be sure to work in the butter thoroughly.

Makes about 30 crackers

1 cup (140 grams) all-purpose flour
2 tablespoons toasted sesame seeds,
    plus 1 teaspoon for garnish
½ teaspoon kosher salt
½ teaspoon sugar
¼ teaspoon baking powder

4 tablespoons cold butter, cubed
1 egg, separated
3 to 4 tablespoons ice water
2 large or 3 small pitted dates,
    diced small

In a food processor, pulse together the flour, 2 tablespoons sesame seeds, salt, sugar, and baking powder to combine and coarsely chop the sesame seeds. Add the butter and pulse until well combined—the butter should be well integrated into the dry mixture. Add the egg yolk and drizzle in 3 tablespoons of the water, pulsing several times until a dough forms. Add another tablespoon if the mixture still appears dry. Err on the side of moist in this mixture, as a dry dough will be difficult to work with. Last, add the chopped dates, pulsing a few times to distribute evenly.

(To make by hand: Combine the dry ingredients, then use your fingers to thoroughly rub the butter in. Whisk together the egg yolk and 3 tablespoons water in a small bowl, then drizzle over the mixture and use a fork to mix until moist clumps begin to form. If it seems dry, add an additional tablespoon of water. Add the dates and stir to combine.)

Dump the mixture onto a clean work surface and shape into a log about 2 inches in diameter. Wrap it in a piece of parchment and twist the ends closed, like a Tootsie Roll, and chill in the refrigerator for at least 30 minutes and up to 1 day. (Any more than 1 day and it will need to be wrapped tightly in plastic to form an airtight seal.)

Preheat the oven to 350°F and line two baking sheets with parchment paper. Lightly beat the egg white with a fork to get a uniform consistency.

Use a sharp knife to slice the log into coins a little less than ¼ inch thick. Arrange them on the prepared baking sheets, spacing them by about an inch. Brush each piece lightly with egg white then sprinkle with a pinch of sesame seeds. Bake for 16 to 20 minutes, until lightly browned on the edges and evenly browned on the bottoms, rotating halfway through. Cool before serving. Stored in an airtight container, the crackers will keep for at least a week.

GLUTEN-FREE NUT + SEED CRACKERS

These thin crackers have roots in the Whole 30 and keto worlds, and I find their assertive, barely sweet flavor to be a welcome addition to any kind of snack spread. They're especially good with winter squash soups or salads that have juicy, crisp components (such as the Celery Salad with Maple-Candied Almond + Shallot on page 169). They have a crisp yet tender texture that can be quite delicate if rolled out super thinly. Using whole nuts and seeds means better, fresher flavor, but if you've got nut and flax meal on hand, substitute ⅓ cup nut meal and a heaping ½ cup flax meal for the almonds and flax, respectively, then grind the chia in a mortar and pestle or spice grinder. This way, you can bypass the blender step.

Makes one 11-by-18-inch baking sheet of crackers

½ cup (80 grams) whole flaxseeds	2 tablespoons toasted sesame seeds
¼ cup (35 grams) whole roasted	½ teaspoon salt
hazelnuts or almonds	¼ teaspoon ground black pepper
1 tablespoon chia seeds	¼ cup water

Preheat the oven to 300°F.

Combine the flaxseeds, nuts, and chia seeds in a blender and process until ground to a mealy consistency—there can be some slightly larger chunks of nuts, but the mixture should be mostly uniform. (On the flip side, don't let the mixture turn to butter.) Transfer to a bowl, add all the remaining ingredients, and fold with a spatula until well combined.

Trim a piece of parchment paper to fit inside a standard baking sheet (11 inches by 18 inches) with no overhang. Lay out a larger sheet of parchment on a work area, scrape the flax mixture into its center, and place the trimmed parchment on top. Using a rolling pin, flatten the mixture until it's uniformly thin and covers almost the entire size of the top piece of parchment. There's no need to be delicate with this dough—you can move pieces around and patchwork them together by pressing with your fingers if necessary. Flip the whole parchment cracker parcel over, peel off the larger top piece, and slide onto a baking sheet.

Transfer the pan to the preheated oven and bake for about 45 minutes, until crisp and darkened a shade. They'll become slightly more crisp once they cool. Gently break them into ragged crackers to serve, and store in an airtight container for up to 2 weeks.

A Few Ideas for Store-Bought Breads, Crackers + Chips

There are lots of great store-bought bread and cracker options, plus several ways to give them a little bit of that "semi-homemade" vibe by *zhuzh*-ing them up a touch. Here are a few of my go-tos.

FRESH BREAD: When bread is good and fresh—whatever kind it may be, whether a whole-wheat boule or a good sandwich loaf—little can be done to make it better. But for textural contrast, brushing slices with olive oil and then briefly grilling them either on an outdoor grill or in a preheated grill pan can introduce some smoky notes and/or crisp texture. Place the oiled slices on the grates of your grill over direct heat, or into a hot, preheated grill pan, for just a few minutes, until they are lightly crisped and take on a bit of color. It's easy to overtoast them in the quest for grill marks; worry less about the grill marks and more about achieving only a light crispiness on the bread. If you like garlic, rub each slice with a halved clove of garlic right after they come off the heat.

DAY-OLD BREAD: Bread that's lost its peak freshness but isn't yet stale can always be re-vived in the toaster. For batch toasting, spread the slices of bread out on a baking sheet and broil for 1 to 2 minutes, then flip and toast the other side. Drizzle with olive oil after toasting. Bread that's gone stale can always be turned into bread crumbs (see page 221) or, if it's still sliceable, into crackers in the style of the Focaccia Crackers on page 187.

FLATBREADS: Store-bought flatbreads—which go by many names around the world, but I'm thinking of the round-ish, pliable, wheat-based ones, like naan, pita, and lavash—can all be improved with heat. Take a stack of them and wrap them in a clean kitchen cloth and then a piece of foil (the foil prevents fire risk, and the towel prevents the breads from oversteaming), place in a preheated 300°F degree oven for 10 to 15 minutes, then keep them wrapped at the table so that they stay warm. You can also warm them in a dry skillet, heat-ing them briefly on each side, and stack them in a clean towel, where they'll stay warm and further soften by light steaming. After they're warmed, consider brushing with oil, melted butter, or ghee, and sprinkling them with a few pinches of fresh, chopped herbs.

PREMADE PIZZA DOUGH: Lots of grocery stores, and even your local pizza shop, will sell premade pizza dough, which can quickly be transformed into crusty, pizza-bianca-esque flatbreads perfect for dips, spreads, and general snacking. Preheat your oven to 450°F, and if you have a pizza stone or steel, give it time to preheat as well; if you don't have one, put an overturned baking sheet in the oven. Divide the dough into baseball-sized rounds and allow them to proof, covered with a clean towel, in a warm kitchen for about 15 minutes, until lightly puffed. Then, working two or three pieces at a time, use your hands to stretch them into rustic rounds approximately 8 inches in diameter. Flour an overturned baking sheet or a pizza peel, if you have one, and quickly slide them into the hot oven, directly onto the stone, steel, or baking sheet, trying not to let too much heat escape from the oven. Bake for 10 to 15 minutes, until puffed and lightly browned. Cut into strips or triangles, or tear at the table.

CRACKERS: When I buy crackers, the first step in my screening process is to look at the ingredients list—I want to see a short one, ideally one that features whole grains, and if there's sugar or other sweetener in the cracker, I'd like it to be at the end of the list. I also find that neutrally flavored crackers are far more versatile in the context of a snacky dinner than those that have distinctive flavor profiles. Last, I also like to play with shapes and textures, combining round ones with those cut into long strips, or large crackers that can be broken into two or three pieces. And it's always good to include one or two gluten-free crackers into the mix. My favorites are rice crackers, rye crisps, the seedy gluten-free ones by Mary's Gone Crackers, and for wheat crackers my very favorites are the artisan-style Firehook Mediterranean Baked Wheat Crackers.

SIPS + SWEETS | DRINKS + DESSERTS

I grew up in a family where the end of the day was almost always marked by a cocktail. Home from work, my parents would retreat to the living room, where they spent a half hour or so debriefing their days while my brother and I entertained ourselves in the backyard. For the longest time, I thought that everyone's parents did this, and it wasn't until much later that I learned how sacred that ritual was for them, and how their friends admired and adopted the same practice in their own relationships.

Similarly, we usually punctuated the end of our meals with something sweet. I realize this also isn't a unique tradition, aside perhaps from our strong commitment to it. But it's one that always stands out vividly in my food memories, particularly the desserts that capped off dinner at my grandparents' house. They weren't ornate or over-the-top desserts. Their meals typically ended with a handful of fun-sized candy bars—Butterfingers, Milky Ways, Crunch bars—strewn in the center of the table once the dinner plates had been cleared. But those items, at least from the vantage point of the kid I was, were no less exciting than a tiered cake or other more elaborate sweet, perhaps because its function was always very clear: it prolonged the meal, and facilitated its most meaningful moments. Time seemed to slow down, and a gentler focus characterized our conversations.

This is to say that in my experience, the tangential parts of a meal can be as nourishing as the meal itself. Certainly, I've had to rein in my enjoyment of cocktails and dessert as I get older, but I'm always seeking to re-create the feelings of those moments of the meal: the pre-dinner cocktail, a firm marker of the transition from day to evening, and the after-dinner dessert, a lingering postmortem on the entirety of the day itself and a final chance to iron out its kinks.

Beyond Snacks for Dinner

In this chapter I've included here some of my favorite desserts for festivities, and they're all "snack"-friendly ones, which means they can be easily eaten out of hand—my "Old-Fashioned" Olive Oil Loaf (a nightcap and dessert in one) or Salted Pistachio Amaretti, in the style of amaretti cookies. But there are also a few simpler sweets for everyday meals, like sticky broiled dates with lime zest and smoked chili, or Toasted Hazelnut + Chocolate Cups, a not-too-sweet little treat to keep in the fridge that reminds me of my grandparents' fun-sized candy bars. And in addition to a few cocktails that might show you new ways to play with plants—Spicy Celery Margarita, or a White (Sesame) Russian—you'll also find some of my favorite drinks that don't feature booze, like Hibiscus + Grapefruit or the Brunch Tonic, both of which are dry, balanced, and not too sweet. I hope the recipes in this chapter figure into your meals, snacky ones and otherwise, bringing ceremony and memories the same way that they have for me.

Sips + Sweets | Drinks + Desserts

BRUNCH TONIC

Here's a fortifying beverage that you probably won't find on any menus but is quite common at restaurants. In a tall glass that's filled to the brim with ice, add a few glugs of pulpy, fresh-squeezed orange juice, seltzer to top it off, and several shakes of Angostura bitters. It's energizing and quenching, a juice-based drink that's more dry than sweet, with the bitters adding some grown-up complexity that might trick you into thinking you're drinking a cocktail. I like to add a splash of raw apple cider vinegar as well, which deepens the tang and even lends some savoriness.

For 1 drink

¼ cup fresh-squeezed orange juice	Seltzer or club soda
1 tablespoon apple cider vinegar	5 dashes Angostura bitters

Fill a tall glass with ice, then add the orange juice and vinegar. Top with the seltzer and Angostura bitters. Stir briefly, then serve.

FRESH GINGER TISANE

I first learned to make this drink in a cooking class at the pan-Asian restaurant Purple Yam in Ditmas Park, Brooklyn. It's an incredibly warming and energizing little sip, the kind of thing I crave when I start to feel sick. I've taken liberties below, adding citrus and honey rather than the traditional brown or black Chinese sugar, because it's evolved slightly for my purposes as a way to kick off a meal. The tea takes just a few minutes to throw together and perfumes the kitchen so beautifully.

Makes 4 servings

1 ounce fresh ginger (about a 3-inch piece)	4 cups water
1 Meyer lemon, lime, or regular lemon	1 tablespoon honey

Use a sharp knife to slice the ginger into thin slabs (no need to peel it). Slice the lemon into thin rounds as well. Combine with the water in a saucepan and place over medium heat and bring to a simmer. Reduce the heat, then partially cover and allow to simmer gently for 20 minutes. Off the heat, stir in the honey, then strain into a pitcher or mugs and serve hot.

HIBISCUS + GRAPEFRUIT, HOT OR COLD

As a nonalcoholic cocktail, I love hibiscus because it has a tannic quality that reminds me of red wine, and while many treatments sweeten it with a heavy hand, resulting in a syrupy consistency that can be delicious, my instinct is to keep all the sour, dry, tangy qualities at the fore. In this way, grapefruit makes a perfect pair. Maple syrup helps to balance the flavors and add a bit of body to the drink, but there's not so much in here as to make it a sweet beverage. When served hot, it's got a festive, mulled wine quality, perfect for holiday gatherings and the like, and when cold, it's a quenching balm for the summer heat. You can usually buy fairly inexpensive loose-leaf hibiscus flowers in bulk at natural foods stores, Caribbean markets (where it may be labeled Flor de Jamaica or Red Sorrel), or online (Burlap & Barrel's Desert Hibiscus Flower is remarkable). If you have them, three blood oranges make a great substitute for the grapefruit.

Makes 2 quarts

2 small or 1 large grapefruit, preferably organic	2 quarts water
½ cup dried hibiscus flowers (20 grams, or 10 tea bags)	Pinch kosher salt
	Juice of 1 lime
2 cloves	3 tablespoons good maple syrup
	Sparkling water or seltzer, optional

Use a vegetable peeler to remove the outer skin of the grapefruit, pressing only lightly to avoid catching too much pith. Combine the skins with the hibiscus flowers, cloves, and water in a medium (3 quart) saucepan, and bring to a gentle simmer. Add the salt and continue simmering for 10 minutes, then turn off the heat and cover. Steep for at least an hour, or until cooled if you have the time. Meanwhile, juice the grapefruit over a strainer (to remove the pulp) and reserve. Strain the cooled mixture into a large jar or other container, and stir in the grapefruit juice and the lime juice, as well as the maple syrup.

To serve hot: Warm the mixture in a saucepan just until it begins to steam. Taste, adding additional sweetener if you'd like. Ladle into mugs and garnish with grapefruit or lemon twists.

To serve cold: Once cool, refrigerate in a large container or bottles until well chilled, then serve over ice. Or to turn it into a sparkler, add ice to a tall glass or tumbler and fill it about 3/4 of the way with the hibiscus drink. Top with seltzer, stir briefly, and serve with a lime wedge.

HERBAL MINT + TARRAGON INFUSION

I know this recipe is almost offensively simple, but I want everyone to be reminded just how quick, easy, and within reach a refreshing, seasonal drink—one that's satisfying and feels special—can be. And it's yet another way to rescue herbs you're not sure what to do with (also see the Herby Seasoning Blends on page 123). Licoricey tarragon and cooling mint work well together, and a short infusion in hot water really helps to unlock their flavor. You can substitute the equivalent of six tea bags of dried mint tea (¼ cup or 4 tablespoons loose-leaf) if you don't have fresh mint, and further lean into the inherent flexibility in this recipe—add a few green tea bags for a stronger flavor (and caffeine), or strips of lemon zest, or start experimenting by adding a teaspoon or two of some brightly flavored whole spices to the herbs as they steep, such as lemony coriander seed, or bubble-gum-like pink peppercorns. I usually prefer not to add any sweetener but have included a lightly sweetened option here.

Makes 2 quarts

1 bunch fresh mint (any variety: spearmint, chocolate mint, etc.)	2 tablespoons honey or agave syrup (optional)
1 bunch fresh tarragon	2 cups boiling water
1 teaspoon fennel seeds, lightly crushed	6 cups cold water

Be sure to wash the herbs by swishing them around in a bowl of cold water to loosen any dirt or debris clinging to the stems or leaves. If the herbs have long stems with no leaves attached, trim those off and discard them, but otherwise leave the sprigs intact.

Place the herbs and fennel seeds in a 2-quart pitcher. If sweetening the tea, add the honey or agave as well. Cover with the boiling water, stirring briefly to dissolve the sweetener if using, and allow to steep for about a minute. Then add the cold water. Transfer to the refrigerator to chill overnight, then strain out the solids. Serve over ice, garnished with mint sprigs if desired.

SPICY CELERY MARGARITA

I don't write cocktail recipes all that often, but I shared this one with readers of my newsletter a few years ago, and it became one of my most popular recipes. It's easy to see why: it takes a perfect cocktail (a margarita) and makes it extra quenching by virtue of an underdog vegetable (celery). Celery is naturally quite salty, so that lends the drink a savory profile, but like cucumber, it contains loads of water, so it also adds a fresh, vibrant juiciness that fully infuses the drink. These margaritas are best made to order rather than scaled up and batched, because the lime juice will oxidize the celery, giving the drink a murky hue (it'll still taste great, though).

Makes 1 drink, easily multiplied

Lime wedge, for rimming the glass
Kosher salt, for rimming the glass
1½ ounces (3 tablespoons) sweetened
celery juice (recipe below)

1½ ounces (3 tablespoons) blanco or
reposado tequila
1 ounce (2 tablespoons) freshly
squeezed lime juice
Celery sprig and lime wedge, for garnish

Prepare the salted rim of your glass by rubbing a cut lime around it and dipping it into a plate of salt. In a shaker filled with ice (or large mason jar, or anything roughly the same size as a shaker and that you can seal), combine the celery juice, tequila, and lime juice. Shake for 15 seconds. Strain the drink over fresh ice into the prepared glass, garnish with the celery sprig and lime, and serve immediately.

Sweetened Celery Juice | Makes about 1 cup

4 long stalks celery, scrubbed and
chopped into 1- to 2-inch segments
1 serrano chili, seeded and coarsely
chopped

⅓ cup sugar
⅓ cup water

To make in a food processor or blender: Combine the celery, chili, sugar, and water in your food processor or a blender pitcher, and blend for 60 to 90 seconds, increasing the speed incrementally, until the mixture is thoroughly blitzed and the sugar is dissolved. Strain through a fine-mesh sieve (or cheesecloth-lined colander), pressing on the solids with a spatula or wooden spoon to extract as much juice as possible.

To make using a juicer: Juice the celery and chili according to your juicer manufacturer instructions. Meanwhile, combine the sugar and hot water in a jar, and shake until the sugar is dissolved, then allow to cool to room temperature. Combine the celery juice with simple syrup—the formula here is 2 parts of the celery-chili juice to 1 part simple syrup.

SALTED PISTACHIO AMARETTI

These cookies, modeled after the Sicilian style of pistachio amaretti, have a pure flavor of nuts and honey that becomes extra delicious with a good dose of salt. The secret here is all about technique: grinding the nuts finely enough to function as flour but not so far that they become butter, adding the correct amount of egg white to bind the dough but not so much as to make it too wet, and then exercising patience while dividing the sticky, vaguely crumbly mixture into cookies. You could roll them in powdered sugar or rock sugar prior to baking for a snowy or sparkly effect, but I don't want them any sweeter than they are. They keep well and are as good with coffee as they are with a nightcap.

Makes about 30 cookies

1 cup (140 grams) roasted, unsalted, and shelled pistachios, plus 30 additional for garnish	½ teaspoon kosher salt
	⅔ cup (135 grams) sugar
	1 tablespoon honey
¾ cup (100 grams) roasted almonds	1 to 2 egg whites

Preheat the oven to 350°F. Line two baking sheets with parchment paper.

Place the nuts in the bowl of a food processor with the salt and process until finely ground, stopping short of it becoming nut butter. Scrape the mixture a few times as you go. Add the sugar and honey and pulse until the mixture is lightly moistened and well combined.

In a mixing bowl, beat one egg white until frothy and doubled in volume, then pour the ground nuts over it. Fold until the mixture just begins to cohere. It will be crumbly and somewhat sticky. To test whether there's enough egg white or not, scoop a rounded teaspoonful and roll it into a ball. It should hold together—if this is impossible, beat a second egg white in a separate bowl, and then fold it in incrementally just until the dough coheres enough to pass the test. It becomes difficult to work with if it's too wet, so try not to add too much egg white.

You can scoop rounded teaspoonfuls of the mixture, roll into balls about an inch in diameter, and arrange on the prepared baking sheets, spacing them out by about 2 inches. However, I find it easiest to dump the mixture onto a clean work surface, divide into two equally sized logs about 1½ inches in diameter, and cut into pieces about ½ inch thick, then roll them one by one. With either method, the mixture will be prone to crumbling. Press a pistachio into the top of each one.

Bake for 10 to 12 minutes, until just darkened a shade—and lightly browned on their bottoms. They'll still feel soft, but will firm up as they cool. Once cooled and stored in an airtight container, these cookies will keep well for about 5 days.

STINGER SPRITZ

In my vaguely agnostic family, one of our few sacred holiday traditions is the Christmas Eve stinger. It comes via my grandfather, who was always in charge of vigorously mixing the drinks until the metal cocktail shaker nearly froze over, and straining them into small, engraved shot glasses reserved all year exclusively for this use. Most everyone recalls their annual stinger with a slight shudder—there was something medicinal about it, and not in a good way. As with many family traditions and their circuitous paths, it turns out that at some point we started making the stinger incorrectly. Its formal recipe is 2 parts brandy to 1 part crème de menthe, but we got the proportions flipped, turning the drink into mouthwash. Once we fixed our error, we realized that the stinger is actually quite delicious! I've adapted the drink here in two ways. First, I've swapped the crème de menthe, which isn't a particularly versatile spirit in my home bar, with anisette liqueur. There's not the same breath-minty rush, but the licorice flavor adds complementary depth to the drink, and the mint leaf garnish provides essential, fresh aroma. Second, I've made it a spritz, which extends the drink, making it more of an aperitif than a digestif—the kind of thing you might be inclined to return to as soon as New Year's Eve, rather than waiting a whole year to shake up another round. To make it traditionally, substitute 1 ounce crème de menthe for the anisette liqueur and omit the simple syrup and soda water.

Makes 1 drink

2 ounces (4 tablespoons) brandy
1 ounce (2 tablespoons) anisette liqueur
    such as sambuca

¼ ounce (1½ teaspoons) simple syrup
  (see below)
Soda water, to top
Fresh mint leaves, to garnish

Fill a tall glass, such as a Collins glass or wineglass, with ice. Add the brandy, liqueur, and simple syrup and stir to combine. Top with soda water—you want about equal parts soda water to the shaken spirits—then garnish with a mint sprig and serve.

How to Make Simple Syrup

Combine equal parts sugar and hot tap water in a jar and shake until the sugar is dissolved.

Toasted Hazelnut + Chocolate Cups (p. 212)

White (Sesame) Russian (p. 211)

WHITE (SESAME) RUSSIAN

This drink came about thanks entirely to the black sesame milk recipe in Amy Chaplin's book *Whole Food Cooking Every Day*. The creamy, toasty, plant-based milk is a delight to drink on its own, but I eventually started to think up new uses for it: cocktails. If the sesame milk is made a little thicker, it takes on the consistency of heavy cream, which brought to mind the White Russian (made of vodka, coffee liqueur, and heavy cream). Substituting the sesame milk for cream, you get a dairy-free dessert cocktail that's tinged with the toasty flavor of sesame. There are a few different coffee liqueurs out there, and their level of sweetness varies quite a bit. I prefer the least sweet of the options, such as Mr Black Cold Brew Coffee Liqueur and Allen's Coffee Flavored Brandy.

Makes 1 drink

2 ounces (4 tablespoons) Sesame-Cashew Creamer (recipe below)	½ ounce (1 tablespoon) coffee liqueur
1 ounce (2 tablespoons) vodka	¼ teaspoon date syrup or agave nectar

Chill your serving glass—this is a drink to serve up, so a coupe or martini glass is ideal, but any small glass will work. Fill a cocktail shaker (or mason jar, or anything that's got a tight-fitting lid) with ice, then add all ingredients and shake for 15 seconds. Strain the drink into your serving glass and serve immediately.

Sesame-Cashew Creamer | Makes about 1½ cups

¼ cup raw cashews, covered in water and soaked for at least 4 hours	1 cup filtered water
¼ cup unhulled sesame seeds, black or white, covered in water and soaked for at least 4 hours	Pinch kosher salt
	1 tablespoon date syrup or maple syrup

Drain and rinse the cashews and sesame seeds, then place in a high-speed blender pitcher, along with the water and salt. Blend thoroughly, then strain through a nut bag or a sieve that's lined with a few layers of cheesecloth, squeezing to extract as much milk as possible.

Rinse the blender pitcher, then return the strained milk to it and add the date or maple syrup. Blend thoroughly again. Pour into a jar or bottle and store in the fridge for up to 5 days.

TOASTED HAZELNUT + CHOCOLATE CUPS

This twist on peanut butter cups falls on the "bitter" end of the dessert matrix, as it's minimally sweetened so as to highlight the earthy, floral fragrance of the freshly made hazelnut butter. If you don't want to make your own hazelnut butter, you can substitute almond butter, but you're missing out. When it comes to chocolate, I encourage you to seek out a fair- and direct-trade brand. (Tony's Chocolonely is one of my favorites.)

These cups must be stored in the refrigerator, because the chocolate isn't tempered. Tempering chocolate really isn't terribly complicated, but it is fussy in that it requires careful temperature monitoring, and is easiest to do when you have a handheld infrared thermometer. Furthermore, the chocolate may lose its shine over time. You can find plenty of tutorials on tempering chocolate online, and by increasing the chocolate to one pound to make a quantity suitable for tempering, it'd be a straightforward process to incorporate in this recipe.

Makes 12 cups

6 ounces dark chocolate (70 percent or higher), vegan if necessary	4 teaspoons powdered sugar
1/4 cup Toasted Hazelnut Butter (recipe below)	1/2 teaspoon kirsch (optional)
	1/4 teaspoon almond extract
	Flaky sea salt, for finishing (optional)

Separate 12 mini muffin cups and arrange them on a plate or small baking sheet. Bring about 1/2 inch of water to boil in a medium saucepan.

If using bar chocolate, chop it into small pieces and shavings with a sharp chef's knife. Place it in a wide, heat-safe mixing bowl, then set the bowl on top of the simmering water. Stir occasionally, using a towel or oven mitt when touching the bowl (it's hot!), until melted. Transfer to a tall, liquid measuring cup with a spout.

Working one by one, pour about a scant teaspoon of melted chocolate into each cup. You can use a small spoon, a mini offset spatula, or even a small pastry brush to nudge the chocolate about 1/4 inch up the sides of the paper lining, but I find it easiest to add the chocolate to the lining, then rotate the cup around on its side. It's important to immediately spread the chocolate up the side of each linings, as it firms up quickly. Once the bottoms are all lined, transfer them to the freezer to firm up, for at least 10 minutes.

In a small bowl, stir together the hazelnut butter, powdered sugar, kirsch, if using, and almond extract. The mixture should be a malleable paste. Roll it into a log. Cut it in half widthwise, then cut each piece in half, and finally cut each piece into even thirds. You'll have 12 evenly sized, disc-shaped pieces.

Mold each disk just a little smaller in diameter than the muffin cups, and set one into each chocolate cup.

Rewarm the remaining chocolate over the simmering water so that it's runny again. Then repeat the process as before, and pour additional chocolate over each cup, enough to seal the hazelnut butter disc inside the chocolate—about ¾ teaspoon. Again, tilt and turn the cups, and even jiggle them gently, to get the chocolate evenly spread over the tops and the sides of the hazelnut butter. Sprinkle the tops with a small pinch of flaky salt, if you'd like.

Return to the freezer for about 30 minutes to firm up, then transfer to an airtight container and store in the refrigerator, for at least 2 weeks.

Toasted Hazelnut Butter | Makes about ¾ cup

1½ cup raw hazelnuts	Kosher salt

Preheat the oven, or toaster oven, to 350°F. Spread the hazelnuts out on a baking sheet, then transfer to the oven and roast for about 15 minutes, until fragrant and darkened a shade. Allow to cool briefly, then rub them against the palm of your hand to loosen the skins—try to get most of the skins off, as they're bitter. Allow the nuts to cool.

Transfer to a food processor and process until the oils are released and the mixture looks glossy, stopping often to scrape the sides and beneath the blade. Add a few pinches of salt to taste. Store in an airtight container in the refrigerator for up to a month.

"OLD-FASHIONED" OLIVE OIL LOAF

For a nightcap, I've always loved the bourbon-based old-fashioned cocktail, a smooth, slow sipper defined by its aromatic floral-bitter edge. This olive oil loaf borrows the cocktail's flavor profile by playing up the orange rind with bourbon and a good dose of Angostura bitters. It also sings with the bright savoriness of olive oil—it's infused with its clean richness and golden color. As an end to snacks for dinner, set out the sliced loaf, cutting each piece in half lengthwise as well for easier out-of-hand eating, or let diners shave off slices on their own. It improves in flavor over time and might even be best after two days.

Makes one 9-by-5-inch loaf, to serve 8

2 eggs	1½ cups (195 grams) all-purpose flour,
2/3 cup olive oil	spooned then leveled
1/3 cup milk	1 cup (210 grams) sugar
Zest of 1 orange, plus ¼ cup of its juice	¾ teaspoon baking powder
1 tablespoon bourbon	½ teaspoon kosher salt
½ teaspoon Angostura bitters	½ teaspoon baking soda

Finishing Syrup

2 tablespoons sugar	1½ teaspoons bourbon
1½ tablespoons orange juice	¼ teaspoon Angostura bitters

Preheat the oven to 350°F. Grease a 9-by-5-inch loaf pan and line with a long piece of parchment paper, with plenty of overhang on either side. Then grease the parchment as well. Be thorough—this cake can stick into the corners of the pan.

In a large mixing bowl, whisk the eggs until blended, then add the olive oil, milk, orange juice, zest, bourbon, and bitters. Add the flour, sugar, baking powder, salt, and baking soda to the bowl, and whisk a few times to blend, then switch to a rubber spatula and fold until the batter is just combined—avoid overmixing it. Scrape into the prepared pan and transfer to the oven to bake until a tester comes out clean and the exterior is deeply browned, 45 to 60 minutes, rotating the pan halfway through.

While the loaf is baking, make the syrup by combining the sugar, orange juice, bourbon, and bitters in a small saucepan over medium heat, stirring or swirling the pan just until the sugar dissolves. Set aside.

Cool the baked loaf for about 10 minutes—it may sink slightly in the center, and that's fine. Run a thin knife around the unlined edges to lift the loaf out of the pan using the parchment overhang and set on a cooling rack. Peel the parchment off, then brush the cake all over with the syrup. Cool completely before slicing. This loaf keeps very well for 3 to 4 days, wrapped in foil.

Fresh Ginger Tisane (p. 202)

"Old-Fashioned" Olive Oil Loaf (p. 214)

DATES FOUR WAYS

My sweet snack is almost always a date—as a dense little treat, they provide sustenance to tide me over. And given that they're a natural vessel once they're split open and the pit is removed, they also present ample opportunity for experimentation. Stuffed with salty or creamy, tangy cheese or nut butter, or showered with lime zest, dates are incredibly versatile. Some of these treatments veer savory, which means you can easily include them earlier in your meal, though I always enjoy desserts that have some salty-sweet contrast, and below are some of the ones I enjoy most. Because dates are so dense, I sometimes find it best to cut them in half (widthwise or lengthwise) for serving, which just extends them a little longer.

Serves 6

Stuffed with Sharp Cheddar and Honey

Use a pungent cheddar here, but one that's got a creamy texture. A hard cheese like Parmesan or a slightly drier one like manchego also works well.

6 dates	Honey
6 pieces sharp cheddar cheese	Coarse or flaky salt
(matchsticks about 1½ inches long by	Freshly ground black pepper
½ inch in width)	

Use a paring knife to make a cut along one length of the date, and then gently pry it open to expose the pit, and pick it out. Place a piece of cheddar in the hollow and gently press the date around it. Arrange on a plate and drizzle lightly with honey, then sprinkle with salt and pepper. Slice in half widthwise to make smaller bites.

Broiled, with Lime Zest and Mild Chili

These are inspired by Chef Ayesha Nurdjaja's incredible version at Shuka, in New York. When broiled, the skins crackle a bit and the flesh becomes sticky toffee.

6 dates	Coarse or flaky salt
Good olive oil	Zest of 1 lime
A few pinches of mild, smoked chili,	
such as Aleppo, Marash, or silk	

Preheat the broiler on its high-heat setting. Arrange the dates in an oven-safe skillet, such as a cast-iron one. Place under the heat source and broil for 2 to 3 minutes, just until the skins begin to blister. Flip the dates, then repeat.

Transfer to a serving plate and drizzle with olive oil. Sprinkle with pinches of the ground chili and salt, and then zest the lime over. Serve warm, allowing guests to pit the dates themselves.

Stuffed with Maple Cashew Cheese

If you don't have homemade cashew ricotta on hand, you can swap in a store-bought cultured cream cheese (such as the Miyoko's brand) or for a non-vegan option a spreadable goat cheese. These dates also pair nicely with savory items—think fruit with a cheese board.

2 heaping tablespoons Cultured Cashew Ricotta (page 89), cultured cream cheese, or goat cheese	6 dates
2 teaspoons maple syrup	Cacao nibs, chopped toasted pecans, or toasted sesame seeds, for garnish

In a small bowl, stir together the cheese and maple syrup. Use a paring knife to make a cut along one length of each date, and then gently pry it open to expose the pit, and pick it out. Divide the cheese between the dates, scooping them into their centers, then gently fold them around the cheese. Sprinkle with the garnish of choice, and serve.

Stuffed with Hazelnut Butter and Chili Crisp

Chili crisp, which is a style of seasoned oil that includes all the fragrant and crunchy solids that flavor it, is becoming more widely available outside Asian markets—the Fly by Jing brand is wonderful, and available through many online retailers. You can use another spicy condiment, such as chili oil, or a hot sauce like sriracha, too.

6 dates	Chili crisp, chili oil, or sriracha
About 2 tablespoons Toasted Hazelnut Butter (page 213), or other nut butter	Coarse or flaky salt

Use a paring knife to make a cut along one length of each date, and then gently pry it open to expose the pit, and pick it out. Fill each date with a spoonful of the hazelnut butter, then gently fold around the filling. Arrange on a serving plate and spoon a little dab of chili crisp on top of each one, followed by a sprinkle of salt.

Salted Pistachio Amaretti (p. 207)

Dates Stuffed with Sharp Cheddar
and Honey (p. 216)

Dates Broiled, with Lime Zest
and Mild Chili (p. 216)

Toast + Jam Blondies (p. 220)

TOAST + JAM BLONDIES

A tub of homemade bread crumbs, made from good bread gone stale, is such a valuable ingredient to have on hand. Throw all your bread odds and ends into the freezer, and once they start to pile up, set aside some time to transform them into bread crumbs. Here you'll use them as a crispy, toasty topping to chewy blondies that feature browned butter, summery fruit jam, and tender whole-wheat flour. The homemade bread crumbs make a big difference, both for their flavor as well as the coarse texture that you can only get by making them yourself. I recommend using a tart jam, such as raspberry or plum, which provides a nice contrast to the deep sweetness of the brown sugar. And I like to store them into the freezer once they're cool—what's good for brownies is good for blondies, too.

Makes about 24 blondies

1 stick plus 1 teaspoon butter

$1/3$ cup coarse, or 3 tablespoons fine bread crumbs (25 grams), preferably whole-wheat (recipe below)

1 cup (180 grams) dark brown sugar

1 egg

1 teaspoon vanilla extract

1 cup (130 grams) whole-wheat flour, spooned and leveled

$1/2$ teaspoon kosher salt

$1/4$ teaspoon baking powder

3 tablespoons tart jam of choice

Preheat the oven to 375°F. Line an 8-by-8-inch baking pan with foil or parchment, leaving some extra to hang over the sides.

In a skillet or saucepan, melt the stick of butter over medium heat, and then continue letting it bubble away until it darkens a shade, smells nutty, and the milk solids have turned a toasty color and sunk to the bottom of the pan. Transfer to a heat-safe mixing bowl and allow to cool slightly. Return the pan to the heat.

In the skillet or saucepan, melt the teaspoon of butter, then add the bread crumbs. Stir to coat them evenly, then toast for just 2 or 3 minutes, until fragrant. Remove from the heat.

Add the brown sugar to the butter in the mixing bowl and whisk to combine, then whisk in the egg and vanilla until smooth. Add the flour, salt, and baking powder, and fold until just combined. Dollop spoonfuls of the jam over the surface of the batter, then fold briefly to swirl it in— the aim is to create streaks, not to blend it into the batter. Then scrape into the prepared pan and sprinkle and gently press the toasted bread crumbs evenly on top.

Bake until the blondies are just set in the center, 16 to 20 minutes. Once cooled, use the foil or overhanging parchment to lift the cookies from the pan, which makes them easy to slice and serve.

How to Make Bread Crumbs

Bread crumbs can be made from day-old bread that's ground in a food processor and then toasted, or you can toast the bread to dry it out, and *then* grind it. The former typically results in coarser crumbs, and the latter finer.

To make coarse bread crumbs: Preheat your oven to 325°F. Tear your bread into small pieces and add to a food processor. It's not necessary to trim off the crusts unless they're particularly chewy, in which case the food processor may not be able to break them down. Pulse as many times as necessary until the bread is broken down into coarse crumbs. Spread them out on a baking sheet and bake for 15 to 25 minutes, checking after 10 minutes, until browned and all the moisture is cooked out.

To make fine bread crumbs: Preheat your oven to 325°F. Spread out slices of bread on a baking sheet and transfer to the oven. Toast until the bread is browned and completely dried out, flipping it every 10 minutes, which will take 20 to 30 minutes total, or more depending on thickness and how moist the bread is. Allow to cool, then break into pieces and add to a food processor, and process until finely ground.

Store in an airtight container in the freezer, they'll keep for up to 3 months.

CARAMEL APPLE + CHEDDAR TOASTS

In these "dessert toasts," soft, caramelized apples are spooned over freshly toasted bread while it's warm, and paired with a slice of pungent, sharp cheddar cheese—a combination I first learned from my grandpa, who always asked for a slab of cheddar cheese with his apple pie. I like to serve everything here as its own component: the warm apples, the wedge of cheese (with a cheese slicer, to make thin slices, if you've got one), and a platter of the toasts. When the cheese is sliced thinly, it softens a little, adding a creamy textural element, but if you wish to honor my grandpa, slice the cheese thickly and serve it cold. Miso adds a subtle savory quality to the caramel sauce, and once you try it, you'll never go back to regular caramel sauce.

Makes 12 toasts

2 firm-fleshed, crisp apples, such as Gala or Fuji
¼ cup sugar
1½ tablespoons cold butter, cut into cubes

2 teaspoons miso paste
12 thin slices of a baguette or other skinny, long loaf
Small block sharp cheddar cheese

Peel the apples, then cut into wedges about ⅛ inch thick: Slice the apples in half through the stem, then carefully trim out the core. With each half lying flat on your cutting board, cut them into thin wedges.

Pour the sugar in an even layer in a medium skillet, then set over medium heat. Cook, without stirring, until the sugar begins to melt and amber-colored patches appear, then gently tilt and swirl the pan until all the sugar is dissolved. Reduce the heat and continue cooking, swirling the pan as needed, until it becomes a mostly even dark amber color—you don't want to burn the sugar, but the darker you can get the caramel without burning it, the more complex its flavor will be. Watch closely. Remove from the heat and whisk in the cold butter, followed by the miso. Return to the heat and add the apples. The caramel will seize up, but it'll soften as the apples cook. Continue cooking until the apples are cooked through and the caramel sauce nicely coats the apples, 25 to 30 minutes, stirring often. Remove from the heat. You can make the apples a day or two in advance—once cooled, store in an airtight container in your refrigerator.

To assemble the toasts: Toast the bread, then rewarm the apples in a saucepan, until the caramel is loose and the apples are heated through, and transfer to a bowl or small, rimmed platter. To serve, set out the apples, toasts, and the cheese, and let guests assemble them: a slice of cheese on the toast, and the warm apples spooned over.

ALMOND CAKE WITH PLUMS
(A WEDDING SNACK CAKE)

This recipe is inspired by the cake that pastry chef Eric See made for our wedding party in the park (page 149). I first got to know Eric as an early and invaluable supporter of *Jarry* magazine, but he's more widely known as a fixture of the New York food and pastry scene, and in recent years he's taken on new notoriety for opening up the New Mexican–inspired bakery and café Ursula, in Brooklyn. He gifted these cakes to Vincent and me for our party, and they were probably the thing that stole the whole snack box show. This is my adaptation of his recipe. His was a marzipan-style almond cake, where butter is creamed into the batter, but I've gone the financier-style route, where melted fat is used. It's got pronounced buttery flavor and a slightly chewy texture, and most importantly, its sturdiness is ideal for snacking out of hand. The cake is flexible in that you can make it up to a few days in advance, and then incorporate whatever seasonal fruit you like as the topping, just before serving.

Makes one 8-by-8-inch cake

Softened butter, for greasing

1 cup (200 grams) sugar

Zest of 1 lemon

1 cup (125 grams) spooned and leveled almond flour

⅓ cup (43 grams) all-purpose flour

½ teaspoon baking powder

½ teaspoon kosher salt

½ teaspoon almond extract

4 large egg whites

6 tablespoons unsalted butter, melted

4 ripe plums, for topping

¼ cup roasted pistachios, coarsely chopped, for topping

Preheat the oven to 350°F. Generously butter an 8-by-8-inch baking pan, and line with two overlapping pieces of parchment paper with overhang in both directions.

In a mixing bowl, use your fingers to rub the sugar and zest together to release the citrus oils, then whisk in the almond flour, all-purpose flour, baking powder, and salt. Use a spatula to stir in the almond extract and egg whites, until well combined. Last, stir in the melted butter. Scrape into the prepared pan and bake until lightly browned and set in the center, 30 to 35 minutes. Cool completely, then use the overhanging flaps of parchment to lift the cake from the pan.

Just before serving, prepare the fruit and arrange over the cake: Slice the plums into wedges about ⅛ inch thick, and then shingle in a single layer over the cake. Sprinkle with chopped pistachios. Use a sharp chef's knife to slice the cake into squares or rectangles.

Once topped with fruit, store in the refrigerator for up to 3 days. Without fruit and wrapped tightly or stored in an airtight container, it will keep at room temperature for up to a week.

A FEW FAVORITE SNACKY DINNER MENUS

Snacks-for-dinner menus don't need to be complicated. The IRL, everyday version of building snacky dinner meals can be as simple as supplementing a recipe you've made ahead with a few hard-cooked eggs, some pickles from the farmers' market, a platter of crudités, and some bread or crackers. It's rare that I survey the table and find that I haven't got all my bases covered when I do this—it just happens naturally when there's variety. But when I'm entertaining or otherwise aiming to impress, I spend some time putting together menus with more intention. I've included some of my favorites—for weeknights as well as for special celebratory occasions. In the weeknight menus, I've led with "anchor" recipe pairings, which form the basis of the meal and can then be further fleshed out with additional snacky items—homemade or store-bought—depending on how many people you're feeding or how big your appetites are.

A FEW SNACKY RULES

Always Include Crudités: They provide vibrant color, quenching crunch, an array of healthy veggies, and set the tone of a snacky meal better than almost anything else.

Include Only One Item that Requires Last Minute Assembly: This ensures that the host can enjoy the meal as well, but also helps to maintain a free-flowing vibe.

Prepare Foods for Eating Out of Hand: This doesn't always work for soups and salads, but any item meant to be snacked on right out of hand should be cut into the correct size in advance. I find two- and three-bite-sized pieces are ideal.

Two—or Three—Dips Are Better than One: If you're going to do dip for dinner, commit to it fully! Be sure to also set out complementary breads, crackers, and other vessels.

WEEKNIGHT SNACKY DINNERS

Lentils, Carrots + Dates with Dill —160
Boiled Eggs with Herby Seasoning Blends—123
Eggplant + Chickpea Whip—98
Crudités —107
    Cucumbers, Small Waxy Potatoes, Radishes or Baby Turnips, Fennel
Toasted or Grilled Bread, or Crackers
Rich Vegetable Sipping Broth —158

Pure Green Soup —168
Australian Zucchini Slice —119
Crudités —107
    Cherry Tomatoes, Celery, Cucumber, Pod Beans, Potatoes
Honeyed Pickled Shallots —62, *or* Olive Bar Antipasti
Stovetop Popcorn —43, *or* Store-Bought Popcorn
Lentil Snacking Granola —36, *or* Roasted Nuts

Squash + Cider Soup —163

Brussels Sprouts with Peanuts + Yuba —162

Grilled or Toasted Bread

Marinated Beans with Sun-Dried Tomatoes—71,
or Lentil Snacking Granola —36

Honeyed Pickled Shallots —62

Crudités —107
Radishes, Cucumbers, Carrots, Celery

Peak-Season Gazpacho with Watermelon—173

Avocado Wedges with Herby Seasoning Blends —123

Lemony Fried Chickpeas —49

Fresh Ricotta—87, or store-bought

Grilled or Toasted Bread

Crudités—107
Sweet Peppers, Cucumbers, Fennel, Gem Lettuces

Elemental Guacamole —102

Crispy Broiled Maitake Mushrooms —50

Toasted Chili–Nut Butter Spread —84, *and/or* Store-Bought Salsas

Soft Tortillas

Tortilla Chips

Marinated Beans with Sun-Dried Tomatoes—71

Spicy Zucchini Quick Pickles —9

Spicy Celery Margarita —206

Cabbage + Tomato Tart in Yeasted Whole-Wheat Shell —133

Celery Salad with Maple-Candied Almond + Shallot —169

Rich Vegetable Sipping Broth—158,
or Prepared Tomato or Roasted Vegetable Soup

Smoky Glazed Pistachios —40, *or* Roasted Nuts

Bread or Crackers

Crudités —107
Cucumbers, Fennel, Baby Radishes or Turnips, Carrots, Endive

Spinach + Ricotta Dip, à la Saag Paneer —126

Oyster Mushrooms in Walnut Oil —68

Gingery Quick-Pickled Beets —64

Warmed Flatbreads

Eggplant + Chickpea Whip —98

Crudités —107
    Broccoli or Cauliflower, Potatoes, Carrots, Cherry Tomatoes

Savory Pear Tart —131

Marinated Goat Cheese or Feta —73

Warm, Revived Olives —74

Crudités —107
    Cherry Tomatoes, Persian Cucumbers, Carrots, Endive

Toasted or Grilled Bread

Stovetop Maple-Ale Mustard —100

Cornichons or Other Small, Zingy Pickles

CELEBRATORY SNACKY DINNERS

Farinata (or Socca) with Chicories —20

Fresh Asparagus Salad with White Beans + Crispy Cheddar —170

Pure Green Soup —168

Oyster Mushrooms in Walnut Oil —68

Crudités —107
    Asparagus, Fennel, Carrots, Celery

Fried Almonds or Cashews with Rosemary —51
    or Roasted Nuts

Crispy Parmesan-Pecan Strips —188,
    or Store-Bought Crisp Crackers

Fresh Ricotta—87, or Store-Bought Fresh Ricotta

Vegetarian Hand Rolls (Temaki Sushi) —135
Crispy Broiled Maitake Mushrooms—50
Gingery Quick-Pickled Beets —64
Gingery Cucumber-Almond Soup —172
Crudités —107
    Allow to Overlap with Hand-Roll Fillings
Gluten-Free Nut + Seed Crackers —194,
    or Store-Bought Rice Crackers

Squash-Sunflower Sliders —142
Crispy Parsnip Fries with Green Chili + Sunflower Seed Romesco —34
Spicy Zucchini Quick Pickles —59
Summer Tomato Salad with Frizzled Shallots —175
Eggplant + Chickpea Whip—98
Crudités—107
    Sweet Peppers, Cherry Tomatoes, Persian Cucumbers, Gem Lettuces
My Ideal Focaccia, or Grilled Bread —185,
    or Grilled or Toasted Bread, *or* Slider Buns

Feta + Jam Tart —117
Roasted Radish + Grapefruit Salad —156
Pure Green Soup —168
Smoky Glazed Pistachios —40
Sesame + Date Slice-and-Bake Biscuits —193
Crispy Broiled Maitake Mushrooms —50
Salt + Pepper Wheat Crackers —190, *or* Store-Bought Crackers
Beer Cheese Gougeres —46
Crudités —107
    Persian Cucumbers, Fennel, Small Waxy Potatoes

Smoky Confit'd Beans with Olives —101
Toasted Walnut + Feta Dip —83
Creamy Sweet Potato Chipotle Dip —97
Gingery Spinach-Tahini Dip —93
Focaccia Crackers —187, *or* Store-Bought Crackers

Gluten-Free Nut + Seed Crackers —194

Crudités —107
    Gem Lettuce, Persian Cucumbers, Assorted Radishes

Chex Snack Mix Revisited —39
    or Sriracha Snack Mix with Puffed Rice + Peanuts —37

Wedges or Blocks of Cheese, Such as Aged Cheddar, Gouda, or Havarti

Lentils, Carrots + Dates with Dill —160
    or Prepared Tabbouleh-Style Salad

Chewy-Crispy Tofu Sticks with Chili-Ginger Jam Dipping Sauce —128

Rich Vegetable Sipping Broth—158

Umami Roasted Tomatoes —63
    over Cultured Cashew Ricotta —89

Baked Brussels Sprouts Chips —45

Crudités —107
    Baby Turnips *or* Assorted Radishes, Carrots, Broccoli *or* Cauliflower, Leafy Herbs

Brussels Sprouts with Peanuts + Yuba —162

Gingery Quick-Pickled Beets —64
    or Store-Bought Asian Pickles

Oatmeal Arancini—140

Roasted Radish + Grapefruit Salad—156

Cottage Cheese Gribiche (With or Without Steamed Artichokes) —105

Mixed Mushroom Pâté —82

Crudités —107
    Fennel, Gem Lettuces, Assorted Radishes, Persian Cucumbers

Focaccia Crackers —187
    or Store-Bought Crackers

Squash + Cider Soup —163

Smoky Glazed Pistachios —40
    or Spiced or Roasted Store-Bought Nuts

ACKNOWLEDGMENTS

Thank you to the team at HarperWave for allowing me into your absolutely lovely publishing family. Thank you, Julie Will and Emma Kupor, for such smart, savvy, and thoughtful edits. Thanks to Milan Bozic for another perfect cover, and Bonni Leon-Berman for a sleek and modern interior design (and navigating the complicated jigsaw of these recipes and photos). Thank you, Yelena Nesbit, for so much tireless and often thankless work in masterminding PR.

Thank you to my agent, Alison Fargis, and the entire team at Stonesong for your continued enthusiasm and advocacy on my behalf.

Thank you to the *Snacks for Dinner* photo team for rolling with the punches through a more-challenging-than-usual shoot: Photographer Cara Howe—you make it difficult to know the difference between work and play since you always show up with your A game and your wonderful company. Stylist assistant (but so much more than that) Paul Wang—it's such a privilege to work with you, and the calm intelligence that you brought to these photo shoots was invaluable; it made everyone do better. Digital tech master Christine Bronico—I'm so lucky to once again have all your expertise on set. Prop stylist Ed Gallagher—it was a pleasure and honor to work with you for a portion of these shoots; I wish I'd had you there for all of them.

Thanks to all of my colleagues at Misen, as it still shocks me that I can get paid while deepening and expanding my cooking knowledge—in particular Omar Rada, Elliott Bell, Alex Mayer, and Trevor Baca Adams.

My longtime family of friends supports me in direct and indirect ways, and it's all incredibly important to me—thank you, Blake Bachman, Meghan Best, Lesley Enston, Crista Freeman, Izzy Forman, Kat Hunt, and Ben Mims. Thank you, Rosie O'Hehir and Emmanuel Rosario, for many delicious and long, lingering meals and shared cooking projects, as well as the wedding party photos that appear on pages 148 and 150. Thank you to the One Chance Fancies (aka my writing group), the first people to provide invaluable feedback on this book idea: Emily Gould, Bennett Madison, Lauren Watterman, and Anya Yurchyshyn. Thank you, Leslie Wooley, who didn't realize she'd inspire a whole cookbook with her seemingly impromptu lunch.

Snacks for Dinner was written during the COVID-19 pandemic, and its influence can't be denied. I was so incredibly fortunate to spend much of it with my brother Max, sister-in-law Casady, and nieces Zoe and Ali, who happened to serve as taste testers on a great deal of these recipes. Thank you to the rest of my ever-supportive family: my first editor/Dad Ron, stepmom Pam, and stepsiblings Anna, Mary Kathryn, and Luke.

And Vincent, who tested every single recipe in this book (oftentimes with me hovering over his shoulder to watch his every movement, in a way that must have been nearly insufferable)—I'm so proud to be your husband. This is just the beginning of what we'll create together.

INDEX

(Page references in *italics* refer to illustrations.)

ABOUT THE AUTHOR

LUKAS VOLGER is the author of four previous cookbooks, including *Start Simple* and *Bowl*. He also cofounded and served as editorial director for the award-winning queer food journal *Jarry*, and previously founded the small-batch, premium veggie burger line Made by Lukas. His accessible, whole foods–based approach to vegetarian cooking has been featured in the *New York Times*; *O, The Oprah Magazine*; *Bon Appétit*; *Time*; and other outlets. He lives in Brooklyn, New York.

For more information, and to subscribe to his monthly(ish) newsletter, visit LukasVolger.com, or follow @LukasVolger on Instagram.